Sharon,

See you at the Top
as a National Sales
Director! Thank so
much for your love
and support!

Love + Belief,
Pat Fortenberry

The principles of Mary Kay Ash are legendary; however, they have taken on a new relevance thanks to the dedication of a generation of women leaders who have lived these principles and passed them forward. Pat Fortenberry is one of those leaders.

David B. Holl
Chief Executive Officer
Mary Kay Inc.

more than *Makeup*

more than  Makeup

by Pat Fortenberry

Mary Kay Independent Elite Executive National Sales Director Emeritus

A Guide to
Finding
Strength and
Leadership
Within You

TATE PUBLISHING & *Enterprises*

Published by Tate Publishing & Enterprises, LLC
127 E. Trade Center Terrace | Mustang, Oklahoma 73064 USA
1.888.361.9473 | www.tatepublishing.com

Tate Publishing is committed to excellence in the publishing industry. The company reflects the philosophy established by the founders, based on Psalm 68:11,
"The Lord gave the word and great was the company of those who published it."

Published in the United States of America

ISBN: 978-1-60462-534-9
1. Biography & Autobiography: Women
2. Business & Economics: Leadership
08.02.13

Contents

Dedication

To my parents Larkin and Ruby Moak, for making me the person I am today.

To my Aunt Ruth Keen, who always taught me that I could be whatever I wanted to be.

And to Mary Kay Ash, who was a leader of leaders, a mentor, an amazing businesswoman and most importantly a friend for me and so many others.

Acknowledgements

I would like to first and foremost acknowledge and thank my husband, Charles, for sharing in this journey of life with me. We have seen the blessings, we have seen the challenges, and we have seen the world. I am glad we have seen them all together; I love you.

I would like to thank my two fantastic children, Pam and Craig, for supporting me while I built my business and understanding that they were my biggest motivation. You have both been an inspiration to me and I am so proud of the woman and man you have become. Pam, the day you debuted on stage as a Independent Senior National Sales Director was one of the proudest days of my life, thank you for being a woman of excellence. Craig, you make me proud everyday and I love to see the entrepreneur you have become. I know you will continue to follow your dreams.

Jacob and Katie, my two beautiful grandchildren, you are the spark that keeps me young and I look forward to traveling the world with you now that I have debuted as an EENSD

Emeritus. I thank God for you everyday, and I am so happy to be your Gigi.

To my brother Richard—thank you and your beautiful wife, Mary Ann for always being there for me; I love you both.

To my son-in-law Chad—thank you for the help on this book; I couldn't have done it without you. You have been a wonderful addition to our family and we love you.

To my faithful assistants Galinda and Shirley—thank you for all of your loyalty, dedication and hard work; I love you both.

Finally, to all of the women that I have had the privilege to meet, learn from, and mentor throughout the years through my unit, the phenomenal Fortenberry Flyers, and my National Area—I wish you all the best and I hope that you know I will always be watching your success as you fulfill all the possibilities you can dream.

Foreword: By
Tom Whatley

Pat Fortenberry chose the title "More than Makeup" for her book for very good reasons. Mary Kay Inc. (the company), Mary Kay Ash (the person), and all of the Independent National Sales Directors who carry on Mary Kay's legacy, are about so much more than makeup. In fact, when asked why she founded her company, Mary Kay's response was always:

> My prime motivation for going into business was to help women. I wanted to provide opportunities for them to create better lives.

Providing opportunities that enrich women's lives is the core of Mary Kay's legacy, and Pat Fortenberry story is a beautiful example of the Mary Kay's legacy in action.

From the time Mary Kay founded her business (Mary Kay Inc.) in Dallas, Texas, on September 13, 1963, thousands of women have created better lives for themselves and their families as they climbed the ladder of success in the Mary Kay independent sales force. Mary Kay was a master in the art of praising people to success and recognizing their accomplishments with diamonds, dream vacations, and pink Cadillacs. Her Company events are legendary in respect to the awards and rewards lavished upon achievers. Recognition was an art form to Mary Kay, and in writing this foreword, it seemed appropriate to first recognize and honor the person whose dream to help women has indeed been a dream fulfilled.

Since 1963, Mary Kay Inc. has grown into one of the largest direct sellers of skin care and color cosmetics in the world, offering opportunities for women in more than thirty markets worldwide. The company achieved another year of record results in 2006, exceeding $2.2 billion in wholesale sales. The Mary Kay independent sales force numbers more than 1.7 million.

By anyone's standards or measures, Mary Kay's company is a business story that can only be described as a "phenomenon." As such, Mary Kay Ash has been profiled on the Biography television channel both in the U.S. and internationally; her business and leadership philosophies featured in numerous books; and her charitable foundation recognized with the Humanitarian Rose Award at a ceremony at Kensington Palace in England. Named the greatest female entrepreneur in American history, by a survey of academicians and business historians across the nation. Survey conducted by Baylor University, her awards and accolades are so numerous that I have listed them separately as a part of this foreword.

To those not familiar with Mary Kay (the person or Mary Kay® products), the fact of such success in so competitive an industry where cosmetic advertising does the selling, begs the question, "How did this happen?" Thus the reason for Pat Fortenberry's book. Pat's story provides a wonderful perspective on how and why this happened. Her story is a beautiful example of what Mary Kay Ash wanted for women. In no uncertain terms and with clearly defined goals, Pat—with the support of her husband, Charles—took Mary Kay's opportunity and ran with it! Her book has but one purpose ... to help others take the Mary Kay opportunity and run with it!

As you read Pat's story, you cannot help but feel her passion for Mary Kay's mission in life and Pat's absolute resolve to sustain the legacy of her mentor, Mary Kay Ash. I can assure you, from the years when I served on the executive team, that the same is true of Mary Kay's corporate staff. She was our mentor as well—always leading by example and teaching us to follow the principles of her business philosophy. Any opportunity to honor her legacy is accepted gratefully; indeed, it is an honor.

Now, let me get back to the business at hand—sharing insights on how Mary Kay's company came to be so successful and, more importantly, why. And why such success will continue in the future. In the early part of her book, Pat reveals her "secret" to success. From my corporate perspective, the secret to the Company's success is that it has had what I call, "Lasting leadership!" I've chosen to focus on the concept of "Lasting Leadership" in Pat's story because in today's world everything seems to be all about change.

Mary Kay believed deeply in the idea that everyone has a beautiful potential that sometimes just needs a little stimulation and encouragement. Her words "you can do it" always brought out the best in others. Mary Kay did not want the spotlight for herself—she focused the spotlight on others.

She built leaders by duplicating herself and taught them to do the same. Mary Kay inspired their potential and taught them to inspire others to develop their potential. Her principles and philosophies, embraced by top leaders, created a succession plan that has truly created lasting leadership. You can follow this plan by reading about Pat's journey—how her start from a scarf and wrong phone number in 1975 developed into the position of Independent Sales Director in 1977 and the coveted position of Independent National Sales Director in 1984. In less than ten years, Pat Fortenberry had developed her potential to become a leader based upon these Mary Kay leadership principles. That these principles would carry on generationally is also evidenced in Pat's story.

Pat Fortenberry and her sister National Sales Directors in the United States and around the Mary Kay world are of one mind as it relates to how they conduct their business—it's the "Mary Kay Way."

Mary Kay Ash shared her business philosophy in three books she personally wrote. First in 1981 her autobiography *Miracles Happen;* then in 1984 *Mary Kay on People Management;* and finally in 1995 a book entitled *You Can Have it All.* All three books became bestsellers, and all three provide a detailed "blueprint" of her rather unique and now proven, highly successful business philosophies.

There is a notation in Mary Kay's book on people management that reads, "Dedicated to all the 'people managers' who still believe that people and pride are the two foremost assets in building a successful business." As you read Pat's book, you will "feel" Pat's dedication to and pride in her people. Mary Kay felt that way about the independent sales force and corporate employees. She often said, "P and L is not about profit and loss, it's about People and Love." Let me ask, how many businesses can you name that espouse this philosophy? Businesses that genuinely respect and build their people instilling pride and dedication to the business purpose?

Mary Kay's business principles do work and remain unchanged since the founding of her company in 1963. Pat's story, like those of thousands of Mary Kay leaders in countries around the world, is living testament to the Mary Kay promise that "You Can Have it All . . ." Pat Fortenberry accepted Mary Kay's opportunity in the same way every single one of the Independent Beauty Consultants have over the years—and still do today. They liked the products and wanted to share them with others. They discovered for themselves the wisdom in Mary Kay's words practicing her leadership principles as they climbed the ladder of success.

Success came to Pat in many ways to a level beyond her wildest dreams. Among the many leaders she has mentored is her daughter, Pam. Talk about people and pride! Pam is an Independent Senior National Sales Director, and Pat's fervent wish is that Pam's success will exceed hers in the years ahead.

Pat debuted as an "Emeritus" in January 2007. In writing this book, she shares experiences gained in a journey of more than thirty years; a journey that led her to the pinnacle of success among the Mary Kay independent sales force. Pat's story offers those with ambitions for their Mary Kay business a track to run on. All the reader has to do is determine a personal destination for herself. Be it a trip to the top or somewhere in between, I hope it is a trip of joy and self-discovery where, according to Mary Kay's thinking, you learn that through giving to others, you *can* have it all!

—Tom Whatley, former President, *Mary Kay Inc.*

Mary Kay Ash

HIGHLIGHTS OF AWARDS, HONORS AND PUBLIC APPEARANCES

2006

* The Biography channel featured a profile on the life of Mary Kay Ash.

2005

* Mary Kay Ash was honored as the recipient of the first annual Trailblazer Award from Women's Enterprise magazine and the YWCA of Metropolitan Dallas.

* Texas Legends Series honored Mary Kay Ash by recognizing her as a Texas Legend for the month of October.

2004

* Mary Kay Ash featured in book, *Around the Corporate Campfire: How Great Leaders Use Stories to Inspire Success.* She is credited as the top corporate storyteller.

* The Wharton School of Business and Nightly Business News named Mary Kay Ash to the list of the "25 Most Influential Business People of all Times" and featured her story in a book with the same title.

2003

* Mary Kay Ash named Greatest Female Entrepreneur in American History from a survey of academicians and business historians across the nation. Survey conducted by Baylor University.

2002

* As part of 40th Anniversary Celebration, a special Pearls of Wisdom CD set released.

* May/June issue of Business Development Outlook magazine featured an article on "Real Losses" of the business community in the deaths of Mary Kay Ash, Stanley Marcus, and Dave Thomas. Each profiled individually.

* Investors Daily, a national newspaper for senior executives, entrepreneurs and investors, featured Mary Key's photograph and an article on its May 24, 2002 cover under the heading, "Leaders and Success."

* Texas Governor Rick Perry signed a resolution regarding the life of Mary Kay Ash.

* Mary Kay featured in book How To Be a Woman of

Influence: Life Lessons from 20 of the Greatest, along with Helen Keller, Mother Teresa, and Marie Curie.

2001

* Women's Advocacy Award, Legal Services of North Texas Inc.

* Mary Kay featured in book, *What's Next? Women Redefining Their Dreams in the Prime of Life*, by Rena Pederson.

* Featured in September *Texas Monthly* article, "Where Are They Now?"

* Mary Kay featured in book, *The Very Best Opportunity for Women*, by Angela L. Moore and Lisa Stringfellow.

* Mary Kay included in the *Feminine Fortunes: Women of the Next Millennium* magazine, an annual publication that honors the achievements of professional women.

2000

* Mary Kay recognized by Lifetime Television Online as the most influential woman in business during the 20th century.

* Mary Kay Ash Charitable Foundation expanded its mission to include programs devoted to the prevention of violence against women.

* One of thirty-nine American women featured in the Unforgettable Women section of The Women's Museum: An Institute for the Future.

* Mary Kay pictured in August issue of Dallas Woman as one of their "Champions of Commerce."

* Mary Kay featured in book, 100 Christian Women Who Changed the 20th Century, by Helen Kooiman Hosier.

* Cover story for The Godly Business Woman, July/August 2000 issue.

1999

* Received Women of the Century award from Women's Chamber of Commerce of Texas, honoring the state's 100 most influential women of this century.

* Mary Kay Ash named "Salesman of the Century" in Texas Monthly magazine's December issue featuring Texans who shaped the state over the past century.

1998

* Mary Kay Ash Cancer Research Institute dedicated at St. Paul Medical Center, Dallas.

* Mary Kay Ash featured in special collector's edition of

Women's Wear Daily as one of six personalities who shaped the industry in the past 100 years.

1996

* Formation of the Mary Kay Ash Charitable Foundation, designed to fund innovative research studies for cancers affecting women and financial support for non-profit cancer organizations for education and assistance.

* Mary Kay honored as one of the Legends of Texas through the "Legends of Texas" Bridge project, Georgetown, Texas.

* Elected to the National Business Hall of Fame by Fortune magazine and Junior Achievement.

* One of twenty entrepreneurs profiled in book *Forties Greatest Business Stories of All Time.*

* Mary Kay published her third book, *You Can Have It All*, which reached bestseller status in a week.

* The National Association of Women Business Owners awarded Mary Kay Ash the Louise Raggio Award.

* *Fortune* lists Mary Kay Inc. among the Most Admired Corporations in America.

* Cover story, *International Business Women.*

* Mary Kay Ash receives National Association of Women Business Owners Pathfinder Award.

* Mary Kay Ash is the cover story for *Women's Enterprise*.

* Feature segment on Discovery Channel's *Amazing America*.

* Featured guest on *CBS This Morning* with Paula Zahn and Harry Smith.

* Featured guest on 700 *Club* with Pat Robertson.

1994

* Profiled in Flare, Canada's premier fashion magazine, February issue.

* Keynote speaker, The Dallas Morning News' Distinguished Women Leaders Lecture Series.

* Featured guest on Hour of Power with Dr. Robert Schuller.

* Financial Television Times Alp Action Award for "Recycling Video."

1993

* Mary Kay Cosmetics included for the first time on the *Fortune* 500 list of the largest industrial companies in America.

* Mary Kay Cosmetics listed for the second time among *The 100 Best Companies To Work For In America*.

* Profiled in *Fortune* feature story, "Mary Key's Lessons in Leadership" September 20 issue.

* Featured in *Free Enterprise* cover story, December issue.

* Dedicated the Mary Kay Museum, a 3,000-square-foot tribute to thirty years of direct selling success; Museum featured on CNN and in other national media.

* Dedicated the Mary Kay Ash Center for Cancer Immunotherapy Research at St. Paul Medical Center, Dallas.

* Dedicated the Mary Kay Ash/St. Paul Medical Center Mobile Cancer Screening Unit, Dallas.

* First female recipient of the Kupfer Distinguished Executive Award, Texas A&M University.

* Keynote speaker, Seventh Annual Entrepreneurial Woman's Conference in Chicago.

* Honorary Chairperson, "Midnight at the Meyerson," Dallas Symphony's New Year's Eve Gala.

* Dallas Mother of the Year Award, Dallas *Can!* Academy.

* Outstanding Texas Citizen Award, Texas Exchange Clubs.

* Appeared on *CBS This Morning*.

* Living Legend Award, Direct Selling Education Foundation.

1991

* Cover story, The Chicago Tribune, Tempo section, February 14 edition.

* Cited for philanthropic efforts by the Variety Club of Texas.

* Cover story in Entrepreneurial Woman, June 9 issue.

1990

* Outstanding Business Leader Award, Northwood Institute.

* National Family Business Award, Baylor University.

* Women of Achievement Award, General Federation of Women's Clubs.

* Business Leader of the '90s Award, Association of Woman Business Owners.

* Individual Komen Award for Philanthropy, Komen Foundation for the Advancement of Breast Cancer Research.

1989

* Sovereign Fund Award.

* First Annual National Sales Hall of Fame Award.

* Circle of Honor Award, Direct Selling Education Foundation.

1988

* Honorary chairperson yearlong Texas Breast Screening Project.

* Featured as Outstanding American Businesswoman on a Korean documentary on the USA.

* Appeared on *Good Morning America* and *CBS This Morning* and featured in "Great American Entrepreneur" series at the Smithsonian Institute.

1987

* Christian Excellence Award in Business, International Association of Women in Leadership.

* Positive Approach Award from *A Positive Approach* magazine.

* Churchwoman of the Year Award, Religious Heritage of America.

* Profiled in *Woman's* Day magazine on family Thanksgivings.

* Woman of the Year, Crystal Cathedral Christian Executive

* Women.

* Appeared on Oprah Winfrey show.

* Distinguished Woman Award, Northwood Institute.

* Honored by President Reagan as one of the women entrepreneurs featured in the National Federation of Independent Businesses Report.

* Ranked eighth in The *Savvy* 60 list of top U.S. businesses run by women.

* Cover story, *Savvy* magazine, June issue.

* Featured in *People* magazine, July 29 issue.

* Outstanding Women in Business in Dallas Award, The Dallas Chamber of Commerce.

* Featured in "America's 25 Most Influential Women" from *The World Almanac and Book of Facts*, 1985 edition.

1984

* Featured in *The 100 Best Companies to Work for in America.*Profiled in Super *Achievers* by Gerhard Gschwandtner.

* Cover story, *The Robb Report.*

* Women's Award of Achievement, Women's City Club of Cleveland, Ohio.

* *Mary Kay on People Management* published by Warner Books; featured on *The New York Times* bestseller list for eleven weeks.

* Entrepreneur of the Year Award, Edwin L. Cox School of Business, Southern Methodist University, Dallas, Texas.

* Appeared on *Good Morning America.*

* Featured as one of the "100 Most Important Women in America" by *Ladies Home Journal.*

* Outstanding Woman of the Year, Les Femmes du Monde.

1982

* Distinguished Business Leadership Award, University of Texas at Arlington College of Business Administration and Advisor Council.

* Appeared on 60 Minutes, Good Morning America, and Late Night with David Letterman.

* Golden Achievement Award from Incentive Manufacturers Representatives Association.

* Named Outstanding Corporate Sales Executive of 1981 by The Gallagher Report, January 4, 1982 issue.

1981

* Business Award for Excellence in Community Service, Dallas Historical Society.

* Cover story, Saturday Evening Post, October issue.

* Free Enterprise Award, San Fernando Valley Business and Professional Association and the Free Enterprise Award Committee.

* Mary Kay by Mary Kay, published by Harper and Row.

* Appeared on The Today Show, p.m. Magazine and Phil Donahue shows.

1980

* Golden Plate Award, American Academy of Achievement.

* Appeared on *To Tell the Truth* television game show.

1979

* Profiled on 60 *Minutes*.

* Appeared on *The 700 Club*.

1978

* Horatio Alger

* Distinguished American Citizen Award, Horatio Alger Association.

* Cosmetic Career Woman of the Year Award.

* Dale Carnegie Leadership Award.

1976

* Mary Kay Ash inducted into the Direct Selling Hall of Fame.

Preface

First and foremost, this book is dedicated to the most wonderful mentor I could have ever had, the fantastic Mary Kay Ash. She had the vision and the fortitude to found a company on the "Golden Rule" of *Do unto others as you would have them do unto you,* and she made it the mission of her life and her company to enrich women's lives. I have lived my life as if she and God are watching me always, and I hope I have made them both proud.

I would also like to recognize Mary Kay's son, Richard Rogers, for taking this Company to heights few imagined possible, for being Mary Kay's right-hand man for so many years, and for continuing her legacy after we lost her. I would like to recognize Mary Kay's family as well for continuing to honor her wishes by keeping Mary Kay Inc. a beacon of integrity throughout the world and proving that a large company can still have a heart and put people before profit.

I would also like to thank Mary Kay's family for growing the Mary Kay Ash Charitable Foundation into an amazing philanthropic organization that raises money to help cure cancers that affect women and supports domestic violence awareness and shelters. To show my gratitude, a portion of the proceeds from the sale of this book will go to the Mary Kay Ash Charitable Foundation.

I would like to thank Mary Kay's Vice Chairman, Tom Whatley, for his leadership and friendship as well as the CEO of Mary Kay Inc., David Holl, for his guidance and navigation of the Company I have loved so dearly.

I would also like to mention my amazing sister Independent National Sales Directors in the Fortenberry Family: Linda McBroom and Karlee Isenhart, who have always made me laugh and have been like sisters to me; Johnnette Shealy, who has been an amazing leader and inspiration; Shirley Oppenheimer, who I loved watching develop into such an amazing leader; my daughter Pam Fortenberry Slate, who has made me the proudest mother in the world; Michelle Sudeth, who defines loyalty and compassion; Vicky Fuselier, who is a leader after my own heart; Kelly McCarroll, whose support and passion have been a Godsend; Scarlett Walker, who drips class and grace; Kimberly Copeland, who redefined success in our business; Rhonda Fraczkowski, who stepped out of her comfort zone and into the spotlight; Donna Meixsell, who has been like a second daughter to me and embodies work ethic; Gena Rae Gass, who sets the bar so high for others; Terri Schafer, who grew up in the business as Shirley Oppenheimer's daughter then took it to the highest level; and finally

Carol Robertson, whose beautiful smile and gracious heart I will miss for the rest of my life.

I would also like to thank all the Independent Sales Directors in my Mary Kay family who have made the journey with me. I cannot thank each and every one of you enough. You have made me a better person for knowing each of you, and you have all taught me so much more than I could have ever taught you. I hope you know—as I put my priorities in order of faith first, family second, and career third—that the line between second and third has been blurred by all of you because you are my family. Through your love and support I have not only made a living—you have given me a life. You have given me a life that I would not trade one minute of with anyone else. My reflections in this book are memories that I will hold fondly as I embark on the next chapter of my life. You have all been an inspiration and I love each of you. I can only hope the lessons in this book can help secure the future of the Company around the world and help others in whatever business they may apply the lessons to. Thank you.

Since the recent death of my father, Larkin Moak, in April 2006, I have been thinking a lot about my heritage. I learned a lot from my parents, and since my father was on this planet for ninety-three years, I believe he had a lot to teach me. I realize now that the success I have experienced in my business is a direct result of the lessons I learned from my mom and dad. I realize that some of the same attributes instilled in me as a child and reinforced by Mary Kay Ash became the cornerstones of my success, and I believe they can translate to success in any business.

* Honesty

* Never settle for anything but your best

* Character—how you act when no one is watching

* Humility—remaining grateful and never forgetting from where you came

* Strive to improve

* Lift up others—make people around you feel important and help others when you can

* Be genuine and sincere

* Be faithful—Jesus said, "If you have faith the size of a mustard seed, you will say to this mountain, 'Move from here to there,' and it will move; and nothing will be impossible to you" . (Matthew 17:20)

* Live your life with discipline

* Always remain a person of your word

* **After I began my Mary Kay Business, I learned the other lessons that have changed my life.**

* Always maintain a positive attitude

* Always think abundantly

* Set big goals and strive to reach them

* Live and work with passion

* Carry a vision of success with you wherever you go

∗ Surround yourself with winners

∗ Expect miracles everyday

I am a product of the attributes instilled in me as a child and the few others I learned on my own. They have helped me carve out a wonderful and fulfilling life for my family and myself, and helped me become a Mary Kay Independent Inner Circle Elite Executive National Sales Director.

It is so important when we have obtained success, whether it is personal or professional—when we have done it with honesty and integrity—that we pass on that heritage. What we have learned is our legacy to those that come after us. Every time I spoke with Mary Kay Ash, she would hold my hand, look me in the eye, and say, "Pass it on." And so I am, as a woman of my word, writing this book so that any advice or wisdom I may have may help someone else on their journey to fulfill their dreams and become the best they can be. I am humble enough to know I don't have all the answers ... but I have a few, and I know Mary Kay Ash will smile down on me as I do as she has asked ... **"pass it on."**

My Journey

As I look back on nearly three decades of the greatest career I could have ever hoped for and the greatest opportunity I can share with anyone, I pause to reflect on what I have learned from all of the amazing people with whom I have shared this wonderful journey. As I reflect, I realize how truly blessed I have been and what a magnificent road I have traveled; a road that has been lined with friends and mentors to guide me and help me traverse the various speed bumps and the occasional pothole. I have to acknowledge that this journey has not been mine alone, and any wisdom I can impart to those who would hear it is not the wisdom of one determined lady, but the accumulated wisdom from those that have helped navigate me to avoid the tribulations they overcame as well as my own insight on the trip. My journey has brought me from growing up with a modest Christian upbringing in the sleepy rural farming community of Bogue Chitto, Mississippi, to being one of the top Independent National Sales Directors in one of the largest sellers of skincare and color cosmetics in the world, Mary Kay Inc. I have gone from living paycheck to paycheck and often having more "month than money" to earning in excess of $9 million in commissions. Whenever people hear what I do the first question they ask is, "You're in Mary Kay? Well do you have a pink Cadillac?" So I have to tell them that indeed I do, and in fact I have earned the use of a pink Cadillac every few years since 1978; fifteen new Cadillacs in all. My life with Mary Kay has not been defined by the money, the cars, the jewelry, or the numerous trips to exotic destinations all over the world (however they are nice perks)—I cherish above all those things the person I have become and the lives I have been able to touch and change for the better as well as the amazing people who have touched my life. Mary Kay Ash told me, "Find something you love to do so much that you would do it for free and then someone will pay you very well to do it." Well, I did.

I guess to appreciate where I am, I should start from where I began. I was born in New Orleans, Louisiana, to Larkin and Ruby Moak. My father had been a Seabee, which means he was a part of the US Naval Construction force in World War II. In the Navy he learned all about telephone lines and equipment. He used his experience when he came home by working for the phone company. My mother, like most women of that era, was a stay at home mom. When I was seven, my family moved back to the town where my parents grew up. I, with my younger brother Richard, lived on a farm in Lincoln County, Mississippi, in a town that is still tiny today, Bogue Chitto. I spent the rest of my formative years in that rural southern town where I attended Bogue Chitto School and graduated third out of the twelve boys and twelve girls in my class, one spot ahead of my then boyfriend and now husband, Charles Fortenberry (I still can't let him forget it). In high school I was very involved in our school's 4-H Club. I actually won a state 4-H Club competition by being able to demonstrate how to make a baked ice cream dish called Baked Alaska.

I grew up in a very religious household. As a matter of fact, I went to church just about any time the doors were open. I enjoyed going to church because when you live in such a small town you look for anything to do, and in rural Mississippi that usually involves the church. I also played basketball and was All-State my last two years of high school, and played for the state championship my senior year. The fact that I even know how to dribble a basketball (let alone that I was really good at it at one time) comes as quite a shock to many people that know me now—especially my grandchildren. As a matter of fact, when I was graduating from high school there was a professional women's basketball team that traveled around and played exhibition games against other local teams. The team was called the All American Red Heads and I was invited to come try out for the team as a defensive player. I never did try out, but it still amazes my grandchildren that their "Gigi" might have had a shot at being a professional athlete, especially now that that they know how much I don't like to "glisten" (I explained to them long ago that ladies don't sweat). But I passed on the opportunity to play basketball to go to college. In reality it wasn't really even an option. I had been raised that education didn't stop at high school. I was expected to go to college. It was actually kind of strange that my parents were so adamant about education at a time when few people actually went to college, including my parents who, aside from a six month stint my father tried at college, didn't have any formal education after high school. But they always instilled in me the need to go to college; many of my aunts and uncles had gone to college so there was never a question whether or not I would go.

When I was going to college the three professions that were mostly available to women were nursing, secretarial work, or teaching. The funny thing about my attitudes when I was growing up was that being a part of sales organization was something I really should avoid. I was taught that it was important to go to college and become a nurse, a secretary, or a teacher, because that was considered to be the normal aspirations for a woman who wanted a career at that time. I knew I could not be a nurse because I didn't have the desire for it, and I didn't want to be a secretary, so I went to school to become a teacher. I attended Copiah-Lincoln Junior College with my high school sweetheart Charles and then transferred to the University of Southern Mississippi. I graduated with a degree in home economics education while Charles transferred to Mississippi State University.

I graduated in June of 1963 and married Charles on June 29 of the same year. Charles had graduated in January, six months early, and had gone to Officers' Training School for the Air Force in San Antonio, Texas. Charles drove straight home from Officers' Training School; we got married and headed out for Chanute Air Force Base in Rantoul, Illinois. That winter I was truly cold for the first time in my life. I had always lived in the South and snow was not something I was used to, but living in Illinois taught me to get used to it in a hurry.

So here I was—newly graduated, newly married, and unemployed in a strange part of the country adjusting to military life and the $220 a month plus housing and a food allowance they were paying Charles to be an officer. I needed a job. A friend of mine got a job with a local school as a physical education teacher and she told me they needed a substitute science teacher. My degree was in home economics education and I didn't know much about science, but I needed a job and they needed a teacher so I stressed the education part of my degree. They overlooked the home economics part and I started teaching high school science. I came home every night and cried. Thank goodness, Charles was a science major in college. He helped me write my lesson plans at night and I managed to stay one-step ahead of my students. But it really was a blessing because they paid me $500 for the month and I was excited; I had become a professional teacher. My next job was as a nursery school teacher. I taught three year olds. It was a far cry from high school science but it was a job. Jobs were hard to find for military wives because the employers knew you would be leaving soon; I had to take what was available.

We soon moved to Altus, Oklahoma, just north of the Texas border. In Altus, I got a job working in a retail shop just across from the courthouse. Being so close to the courthouse, we would hear about different government jobs that were coming open. One day I heard of a posting for a social worker job; I went, applied, and took the Civil Service examination. A short time later, I was hired as a social worker working with foster children. I loved my job. My boss was a great guy and I loved the people where I worked—I actually felt like I was doing something worthy. People use to ask me when they heard I worked with foster children if I thought it was sad taking children out of their homes; it was. But knowing the situations I was getting those kids out of, I was honestly sadder when I had to take them back to a bad situation, which I often had to do. I used to think I was tired from working that job because I would get home every day and fall asleep for an hour; once I changed jobs I realized that I had actually been emotionally spent most of those days. To this day my hat is off to social workers and the job they do.

I left social work when a position opened for an Extension Home Economist for the county. I finally had a chance to use my degree. I applied for the job and got it. I loved working with the local 4-H Clubs and helping the ladies that did home demonstrations. My boss and longtime friend, Pat Coffey, was wonderful. I got to travel and even had a spot on a weekly radio show talking about the upcoming home economic events in the area. It was a great job for me and I guess my star was really on the rise there—when there was a possibility of us leaving, my bosses really tried to persuade Charles to get out of the Air Force and settle in Oklahoma so I could stay on as the Extension Home Economist.

But Charles really wanted to pursue his career and become a pilot so we moved to Craig Air Force Base near Selma, Alabama. We knew we were only going to be in Alabama for a year, which was not enough time to get a job, so I used that time to work on my suntan. We lived in a tiny apartment near the pool and I spent time playing bridge or swimming at the pool. The next year, 1968, we moved to Buzzard's Bay, Massachusetts, and my first child, Pam was born. With the Vietnam War raging and Charles serving tours of duty there, he and I decided that I would stay home and raise Pam. During this time, we were stationed in Okinawa, Japan, and I was introduced to the Asian culture for the first time. I enjoyed the experience and the introduction turned out to be a blessing later in my Mary Kay Business. Charles was stationed stateside in 1971. I was a stay-at-home mother of one until 1972 when I became the stay-at-home mother of two with the birth of my son Craig in Langley, Virginia.

Why Not Me?

In 1975, Charles, and I were living in Montgomery, Alabama, where the United States Air Force had stationed us because Charles was an up and coming officer and a pilot. I had graduated from the University of Southern Mississippi, worked as a teacher, a home economist, a social worker and even had a small part on a weekly radio show for a short time. But I was now a mother of two, my daughter, Pam, and my son, Craig, who were six and three years old respectively. As parents, Charles and I believed it was important for me to stay home and help raise the children. While I do believe it was the right decision at the time, I must admit—being a stay at home mother for six years wore on my self-esteem and my confidence was at an all time low. I had moved many times since I married and it was time for us to be transferred again. So in March, as we were in the process of selling our home in Alabama, I noticed that many of the women who came by to look at the house had remarkably beautiful skin. I was at an age when it is normal to get curious about fighting the contours that creep up on you. I began asking them what kind of skin care they used. They all had the same answer: Mary Kay® cosmetics. Soon after, I was invited to a friend's house for a Mary Kay® facial. I was honestly rather excited to go because my social calendar was not full. When you spend all day talking to toddlers, as I am sure many of you know, you really begin to crave adult conversation and company. When the day came for the appointment, however, life was in the middle of happening, and I forgot all about the skin care class. When my friend called with a reminder about the class, checking to be sure I would be able to make it, all I could do was scoop up Craig and hurry over. I was not about to miss my one chance that week to get away from laundry and children's shows.

Once I saw the class I was hooked. I was so impressed that I scheduled a class of my own for a few days later. When I hosted the class, the Beauty Consultant went through the class and we all cleaned, primped and admired. I was just as enthusiastic about it as anyone. Imagine my disappointment when, at the end of the beauty class, when I was sitting there with the most thorough makeover I could do on myself and feeling the best I had felt in weeks, the Beauty Consultant I had hosted the party for asked my best friend if she would like to become a Beauty Consultant—but never bothered to ask me. Honestly, I was a little jealous and hurt that she thought my friend had what it took to become a Mary Kay Independent Beauty Consultant but not me. But I never said a word. I began using the product and loved it. The Consultant who sold me my first product moved and a couple of months later Charles came home from one of his master's degree classes and said, "I think I have found the perfect job for you." A new

Beauty Consultant in his class was going on and on about this new cosmetics company, Mary Kay Inc. She told him the whole philosophy behind the company: faith first, family second, and career third, and no territories. I could go anywhere in the country to sell and recruit without having to give up the business I had already built. I wasn't really looking for a job but if I could work a few hours a week and make some extra, much needed money, I wanted to look into it.

Thankfully, the lady in my husband's graduate class had painted a wonderful picture of the Company and the opportunity to him, and he was able to persuade me without too much prodding to go and listen to the marketing plan and give Mary Kay® one more chance. I signed my Mary Kay Independent Beauty Consultant Agreement that day at the home of Independent Senior National Sales Director, Pat Danforth. She was an Independent Sales Director-In-Qualification at the time, and the check I gave her was for money we didn't have for extraneous expenses. Thankfully, the check cleared and I was a new Mary Kay Independent Beauty Consultant, and a lifetime of dreams has been fulfilled and wishes have come true from that starter kit. I am so thankful to Pat Danforth for giving me the encouragement I needed to sign my Mary Kay Independent Beauty Consultant Agreement; surely, my life would have been very different if she hadn't. Thank you, Pat. I often think back to that first Beauty Consultant and how her business and possibly her life may have been a little different if she had followed Mary Kay's wishes and shared the opportunity with everyone, including me. Since then I have remembered how I felt when I wasn't asked to be a Mary

Kay Independent Beauty Consultant at my skin care class and have made it a point to never miss an opportunity to share the Mary Kay opportunity with everyone when I am conducting Mary Kay business, no matter how shy, successful, perfect, or imperfect their lives seem to be—it is not up to me to decide if a Mary Kay business is right for them. It is their choice. I can share with them how wonderful a decision it has been for me and let them decide if it might be right for them. I have made a lot of wonderful and lifelong friends that way.

I went home a new Mary Kay Independent Beauty Consultant and I was so excited. The first thing I did was call my best friend. I told her that I was starting my very own business selling Mary Kay® Cosmetics; I truly thought she would be happy for me. I waited for a second and all I heard was, "Oh Pat, what do you want to do a thing like that for?" The disdain in her voice almost broke my heart. So when I hung up with her I turned to the person who I could always talk to besides my husband—my mother. I told her my exciting news with a little less wind in my sails after the conversation I had just had with my friend. My mom said, "Four years of college, Pat, and you want to peddle lipsticks?" By the time Charles got home, I was about ready to quit my business before I even got started, just because I listened to a few negative comments. Thankfully, Charles said, "Those people don't have to do this business, it's your business, you're the only one that has to believe in it."

He was right, and he still likes to hear me say it. He gave me the inspiration to move forward and we are both still glad he did.

Who Me?

Soon thereafter we moved to O'Fallon, Illinois, a small town of 6000 people just across the river from St. Louis, Missouri. I did five classes during the move; three in Montgomery, Alabama, and two in Mississippi.

There I was, a homemaker from a tiny town in the Deep South, newly relocated to the outskirts of one of the largest cities in the Midwest without a friend or extended family member within five hundred miles. Now I had to find some faces other than my own to try the product. Miriam Alexander, my adopted Sales Director, comforted me by telling me, "Don't worry, Pat, strangers are just friends you haven't met." I did what my first instinct was then and still is now—I went shopping. I had ten extra dollars that I could squeeze out of our budget. I decided I needed a scarf. I went to the mall and soon found a scarf in my budget. I went up to the checkout and began talking to the cashier and I asked her if she had ever heard of Mary Kay Cosmetics. Her answer was no, which wasn't unusual back then, so I blurted out, "Well, *you wouldn't want a facial would you?*" Now we all know that is not how we are taught to share the product or sell anything. It was hardly coherent, let alone good salesmanship. So imagine my surprise when her answer was yes! I didn't have any business cards, but I did have a slip of paper and a pen; I got her name and phone number and went home pondering how long I should wait to call as to not sound overly eager.

The next day I was pouring over all my leads from the previous days' prospecting and no matter how many times I counted, I still got the same number—one. Since my options were limited, I decided to call my cashier acquaintance to book the facial. It was a wrong number. To this day I don't know if she gave me the wrong number or if I wrote the wrong number down, but the number I dialed was not hers. The voice on the other end of the line was a woman and I assumed she had skin so I stepped out of my comfort zone. After I had explained everything that had happened that brought me to that point with her on the phone, I made her the same offer I made the cashier.

"You wouldn't want a facial would you?" To my surprise she said yes too. I booked a facial with the wrong number, held the facial, and sold a basic skin care set for $21.00. I left with a $10.50 profit and follow up appointment for a week later. I had started my Mary Kay business. I held my follow up appointment with my new and only customer and three of her friends, sold some more product, and booked some more classes. I was off and running.

Six months later I was headed to my first big Mary Kay event—the January Jamboree in Chicago, Illinois. That is where I caught the vision. I heard Dalene White, a National

Sales Director, tell us about the fantastic commissions she was making. I was astounded. I started my Mary Kay business to make an extra $100 a month so I wouldn't have to pilfer the grocery money to buy Pam's Easter dress. That's when I changed my goal. At that second I knew I wanted to be a Sales Director, and I knew I could make $1,000 a month. Then I heard Mary Kay speak and I changed my goal again; I would be an Independent Mary Kay National Sales Director and spend the rest of my working life building my Mary Kay business. When I went to that Jamboree, I was working a business; when I left, I had a vision for my future.

I returned to Chicago the following January of 1977 and debuted as a Sales Director on stage. A year after becoming a Sales Director I received my first $1000 commission check. By Seminar 1984, my unit was the top unit at the Sapphire Seminar, where I debuted on stage as the 58th Mary Kay Independent National Sales Director. More than twenty years later I have earned more than $9,000,000.00 in commissions—all from a scarf and a wrong phone number.

My Secret

If any of you reading this book are hoping that I am going to unveil the secret to my success, to give you the magic formula that will unlock the treasure chest in your life and enable you to accomplish everything that I have and more—then you are in luck. I am going to give you my secret here in the first chapter and you can take it and run with it. You may not even need the rest of the book. Everything I will say will only come back to the underlying theme and strategy I have used to become a multimillionaire. This strategy has worked for me from the very first day I learned it, and has helped me navigate the trials and tribulations of not only my business life but my personal life. This secret was taught to me when I was very young and still in Bogue Chitto, Mississippi, and has guided me since then and has led me to where I am today. I would not even dare to think where I would be if I had never learned my secret to success. But unfortunately, I know there are millions of people who have never heard my secret and I am counting on you to share it with everyone you meet. I have shared my secret before, I have seen it change people's lives instantly, and now I am going to share it with you.

Unconditional Love.

That is it. You don't have to write it down; you probably do not even have to do much work to remember it. But it is the secret that has guided me through my entire life and my entire business. Once you implement my secret, the world will unfold for you. You can have everything you want financially, emotionally, and spiritually, and you can be anything you want to be with unconditional love.

I believe that our natural state is to be loved and to share love. Our bodies and souls strive and thirst for it, and we see the need for it everywhere we look. In every crime, in every conflict, in every sad story you can see where unconditional love can help. I have always heard the expression, "Love makes the world go 'round," and I can say without a doubt that it is true. But even more amazing to me is that love can do anything, inspire anyone, and overcome any obstacle. I can tell you without a doubt that I have loved each and every person that has touched my life, and I have loved them unconditionally. Of course, I have different kinds of love for my husband and my family; but the unconditional love, like the love God has for us, I pass on to everyone who enters my life. Because of this love I believe that I have attracted the people to me in my life that have made me who I am and have helped me to reach the level of success that I have achieved. I have been amazed at the power of taking a small piece of my time, sharing unconditional love with a virtual stranger, and seeing the spark that lights up their eyes. I have seen that spark turn into a flame and burning desire to do more and be more than they ever thought possible. And I have seen them go on to spread their own love and ignite that spark in others. That is my big secret, and I will put it up against any business plan or "get rich quick" scheme as a recipe for success. Mary Kay Ash always told me, "No one cares how much you know until they know how much you care." I have built my life and my business on that very concept. When you give unconditional love, people respond. People want to be around you when you give unconditional love. They want to help you reach your goals because our very nature is to nurture and lift up those who give us love. It is the reason a child listens to a parent or the way a caring teacher can turn a struggling child into an Honor Roll student. When you are giving unconditional love to everyone you meet, that is thousands of people lifting you up. I am not saying that every person you meet will quit what they are doing and devote their life to helping you achieve your goals. What I am saying is that when you give unconditional love it will come back to you. Perhaps it will be just a stranger holding a door open for you when your hands are full or a smile as they pass you on the street, but it all comes back to you. And occasionally you will have people that will drop what they are doing and help you reach your goals! The reason it comes back to you and the reason it will make people want to lift you up is because it is contagious. When others learn to give love unconditionally, they will find people lifting them up and the cycle continues.

The best thing about my secret is that it is foolproof and limitless. You cannot run out of unconditional love, and no one can use it all up and create a shortage somewhere else. You cannot be hurt by giving unconditional love and you cannot hurt anyone else by giving it to them. There is absolutely no downside to it! You can impact someone's life so dramatically that you can change the very course of it for the better. I believe we have a battery inside of us that is charged by love, and the wonderful thing about this battery is that it doesn't care which direction the love is going to get fully charged. If you encounter someone who gives you love then your battery gets charged, but it also gets charged every time you give love. If you don't believe me just give it a go. Walk down the street or around your office or around where you live and muster a genuine feeling of unconditional love in your heart; when you encounter someone, smile and give them a kind "Hello," or "Good Morning," and in your heart project that love to them. Not just the people you think look nice or look like they are looking for someone to talk to, but to everyone. Project unconditional love to everyone in your space because *unconditional love does not judge and is not selective.* You can look at everyone you come into contact with and make a list of

(*unconditional love does not judge and is not selective.*)

everyone who does not need or want more love in their life; I assure you at the end of the day, the month, or the year, your list will be empty. Some people may look at you like you are crazy, some people may ignore you and walk on past. Some people may actually say something rude to you. It does not matter. Because when you are walking around with a genuine feeling of unconditional love in your heart, you are charging your battery every time you give it away. You will probably just laugh to yourself a little at the people who you don't think acknowledged your love and keep on going, but they felt it. They might not know what it was, but their battery got a little charge, and it will come out as a smile eventually. If they choose not to accept your unconditional love then you get the benefit from expressing it; they will go on with a little charge and maybe it will lead to more, and if they were rude to you then they need it the most. But most exciting is that eventually, someone will respond with a warm greeting back to you and you will both get a big charge—giving and receiving unconditional love at the same time will keep you going, making it all worthwhile.

What comes next is the best part. As you keep giving unconditional love, it builds like a snowball rolling down a hill. It rolls slowly at first and you might get a warm greeting from a stranger or a hug from a friend that feels extra special. But as you give it more and more you will notice it build and build. You won't even be thinking about it, but you will be radiating unconditional love to everyone around you. People will seem friendlier, you will get compliments for seemingly no reason, and people will want to be around you more just to be in your space. Unconditional love is an attracting force because everyone wants it, everyone needs it, and everyone craves it. You can ask the richest man in the world if he is happy and if does not have love in his life then he will certainly answer no.

So there you have it; my multimillion dollar secret. It actually is not much of a secret. I have given unconditional love to probably hundreds of thousands of people in dozens of countries during my lifetime. And if I did not have a penny in the bank I would still be rich because it has come back to me a hundred fold. I was taught my secret by my mom and dad and it was the greatest gift I have ever received. I have done my best to pass it on. I have given unconditional love to people who don't even know what I'm saying because they don't speak English, but they understood it. Unconditional love is the true universal language and I speak it everywhere I go.

What Makes a Leader?

Throughout this book I have and will talk about what I have found that makes people successful. I believe that unconditional love can truly make the world go 'round, but without direction it wouldn't know which way to spin. Along with unconditional love, I have learned one thing that makes people more successful than anything else, whether that success is personal, financial or spiritual—developing leadership. If you want to lead an army of thousands or you just want to be in control of your own destiny, everyone has to learn to be a leader. We are leaders as parents, as teachers, as coaches, and as friends. How we use our leadership and how we grow our leadership qualities can help us in every walk of life. But how do you become a strong leader? You build yourself into one.

One of the most important things Mary Kay asked of her Independent Sales Directors and Independent National Sales Directors was to continue building leaders so that our company will continue to grow into the future. I want to share with you a list that Mary Kay shared with me.

She said good people become good leaders because:

* Leaders are disciplined people.

* Leaders are easily self-motivated.

* Leaders accept personal responsibility for their successes and failures.

* Leaders set themselves apart by striving for excellence everyday. Everyone makes mistakes but leaders strive for excellence despite those mistakes.

* Leaders are flexible.

* Leaders know everything has a price tag paid in personal effort. Nothing is free, not even failure—enjoy the price of success.

* Leaders know the value of enthusiasm. They are excited and it shows. After all you can't have enthusiasm without the ending–iasm, which I believe stands for:
    I-I
    A- am
    S- sold
    M- myself

* Leaders make others feel important.

* Leaders think about what they say before they say it. They understand the power and effect of words.

* Leaders are Goal Setters; they set goals and work them through until they are completed. They take the ups and the downs and stay the course. They know deadlines may change but the goal remains the same.

* Leaders handle their emotions with intelligence and common sense. They dump the drama and choose to live a victimless life. (Act on your will not your emotions.)

* Leaders find a way—they don't give up easily.

* Leaders want to succeed. Always remember, they have a desire to be better. Their success isn't being better than anyone else, it is being better than they used to be.

* Leaders are not always in a crisis. Leaders don't have problems, they have situations with solutions.

* Leaders accept and seek responsibility cheerfully. They have a "whatever it takes" attitude. There is a difference between what is required and what is inspired.

* Leaders have a positive attitude and work to keep it.

* Leaders do not gossip.

* Leaders keep their word. They under promise and over deliver.

* Leaders lead their people by their own example and never expect their people to do anything they are not willing to do themselves.

* Leaders are never critical or sharp spoken.

* Leaders show up suited up and ready to go, no matter what the circumstances are.

* Leaders carry the vision of where the team is going. They are the keepers of the dream.

* *Leadership is developed daily, not in a day.*

So before you can develop others into strong leaders, I think you must develop your leadership qualities first so people will want to be like you. The good news is your past does not equal your present, and your present does not equal your future. You can change your life with a decision. You can make a decision today that can change your behavior and therefore change the course of your life forever. The potential for leadership lies within all of us, but the development of that potential to a higher level remains locked in many people.

To climb to a high level of leadership takes commitment, not just for a year but for the lifetime because it is a constantly unfolding process. As you learn to develop leaders, you become a better leader yourself.

Growing into a leader takes several things.

* A belief that you have the gift of leadership within you.

* A willingness to do what it takes, over and over.

* A willingness to accept responsibility for your success

or failure and not getting into a pity party and not blaming others when you slip up. You must learn "bounce back-ability" and shortening the time between a set back and the next goal.

* A passion to grow and learn—school is never out for the pro.

* A desire to make a difference in the lives of others.

So how do we bring this out in ourselves and in others?

First let's talk about the gift of leadership lying inside you. Take a bag, any bag—it could be an old purse or a grocery bag—and set it in front of you. I want you to envision that bag holds an unwrapped gift—the gift of your potential. Close your eyes with that bag in front of you and imagine that you can reach into that bag and pull out anything in the whole world. It could be anything from a $0 balance on your credit cards to a college education for your children to your own private island in the Caribbean! You only have to believe in your own potential. You have to not guess but know that there is not anything in this world that you cannot achieve with enough effort and fortitude. It is said that at best we only use about one-tenth of our brain's potential. I contend that this statistic isn't limited to just our brain's potential. I believe it is all of our potential. So, if there are people going to the moon or becoming billionaires from nothing, imagine what you could do if you used more of your potential! Aren't you curious about the other 90%? To become an outstanding leader you first must believe in your talent.

Have a curiosity to discover your own potential. God put the seeds of greatness inside all of us, not just some of us.

The second part of the evolution into a great leader comes from a willingness to do what is needed to grow. This can be the easiest and the hardest part because the activities do not change—that is easy. Whatever it is that you do in your business or personal life that brings you success—do it! If it's working out, praying, or making sales calls...you know what gets the results you want. Doing them over and over can become repetitious or boring. But when we stop doing them, we release our personal power and become a manager not a leader. We manage our shortcomings instead of maximizing our potential.

The third part of your evolution is to maintain small and large goals that keep you focused, committed, and excited. This also keeps your people focused. Never should one goal be met without knowing what the next one is. I have known so many people who have completed a big goal and then stopped. Before you know it they are wallowing in self-pity because they have lost momentum and things are going backwards. This scenario does not happen when the goals overlap. Sometimes, when we start going backwards it becomes easy to blame others for the slip up. Often we tend to blame those around us. Whether it is family or coworkers, it is easier to blame someone other than ourselves when we fail. But a leader looks to take responsibility as readily for their shortcomings as they do their successes. The people around you can support you if you put the goal out for everyone to see, but if you stop doing the daily things it takes to reach the goal, it is likely that those around you will lose sight of the goal as well.

So how do you prevent this? The people around you need a goal of their own just like you do. For a short time people will work for the goal of the whole group until they find their own passion. So it is important to have a goal in place at all times that will help those around you to stretch and grow the unit until their individual passion is found. As people see others reaching goals around them their pride grows because of being part of it. Everyone wants to be on a winning team.

The fourth part of leadership is developing people skills. The better you understand and get along with people the faster you will move forward.

What are these people skills?

* Start seeing the potential in others and let them know what you see. It must be honest and sincere because people can feel it when you are just talking the talk. When you truly see their potential, they feel it and they learn to trust you. Without trust you cannot develop them.

* Make people uncomfortable. They have the same untapped potential and talents that you have and most of them do not believe in it—they need to be stretched, first with small challenges and ultimately with bigger ones. Keep showing them what is in it for them.

* Recognition. Everyone loves to be recognized. Even tiny accomplishments, when they lead to recognition, can lead to great things. Do you praise your people in

front of others? Do they take part in your meetings? Do they get calls, notes, and emails congratulating them on their efforts? If they don't they should. As a parent we call it positive reinforcement, but everyone loves it, not just our children.

* Follow up. No matter what you do, it is worthless without immediate follow up. True leaders are masters at follow up.

* Accountability. Make sure you are accountable to someone who will expect you to complete your commitment. The people you lead should be accountable to you as well! You are the role model for achievement. Remember, they know when you are not setting goals.

* Create an educational path for develoing leaders and stick to it, year in and year out.

* Showcase people. Good leaders share the limelight. In fact a good leader is more focused on giving recognition to people than she is in getting attention for him or herself.

How do you make people feel? You may want to stop just talking to people, start looking at them more, listening to them more, and praising them more. Think carefully before you say something to them, especially if it is advice. Mary Kay Ash never criticized her people, but when she needed to correct them she layered the correction with tons of praise for what they did right. The people who were taught by Mary Kay always remembered her care and concern with this manner of communication and no one ever got hurt in the process.

* Do not take responsibility for another's failure or success. Your responsibility is to recognize people with potential and offer them an incredible opportunity. Your responsibility is to also educate these people, to be a proper role model for them, and believe in them more than they believe in themselves. The rest is up to them. They may walk with you for a block or for a mile or even a lifetime. Some will stay, others will leave. No matter what they choose, if you have done your best, you can be proud of what you offered them. Take pride in the opportunity you have to give. It is your greatest gift to give.

* Daily, you will want to commit yourself to activity that will develop you as a leader. Every time you pick up the phone or head to the computer, ask yourself, *Is this going to help me to become a better leader?* Leadership is about inspiring yourself or others to activity and thus your daily activity must meet that definition.

* Most businesses are about constantly searching for your next leader; note the words "your next leader." It is not up to the people in an organization to produce a leader. Sometimes leaders make themselves known, other times it is our responsibility to find and nurture them. It has been proven that leaders select people with more potential than their own. So if you have an instinct about someone's leadership ability, follow it.

You can choose a leader because you have worked to become one.

The fifth step in your elevation of leadership development is a desire to help others through your vision.

Imagine yourself as a leader with a great vision and a plan to live that vision. Mary Kay Ash told us that others will follow those who *do*, not those who just say what to do. Be a coach whose team shares that vision and dares to dream.

Dare to dream; to fear is to fail. How much of a risk taker are you? Will you travel far and wide? Will you take on more tasks than ever before, believing that you can handle more? A leader goes the extra mile, every time. Just like the runner that leads and wins the race, they did not get there by sitting on the couch watching TV. They taught that little bit extra every time.

Mary Kay Ash was the biggest risk taker I've known. She spent her entire life's savings starting a company that had a design for success that so many have profited from. We can all be like Mary Kay Ash or Arthur Ashe or JFK or Gandhi— influencing more people than ever before. Are you a proud leader of an outstanding team of winners? As their coach, do you inspire them to use all of their potential, not just monitor their tasks and skills? A partner for success gives more, respects more, believes in his or her people, and expects action now!

As a leader you'll want to walk the walk and expect no less from all those you lead. Live a life of positive expectation and people will want to be around you, follow you, listen to you, learn from you, and let you coach them to find their inner power. You can be a prisoner of your past or a master of your future. Your future belongs to you, and only you hold the key.

As you are forging yourself into a strong leader, you will find the strength in yourself to see leadership qualities in others. Then you can put your leadership to work and help them break out of their shells to become leaders themselves.

Duplicate Yourself

I think I am pretty good at what I do. I do not say this out of conceit. It is the conclusion I come to after evaluating the success I've had, and the people I have influenced after the tremendous amount of work I have put into my business. But I can say with one hundred percent certainty that I could not have achieved what I have on my own. I would also suggest that whatever business you do, the amount of success you will have will be limited if you attempt to do it all yourself. And since you are the one who knows best how you want your business to look, who is the best person to get to help you run your business? *Another you!*

Any successful business has a culture. The culture is a core set of values or beliefs that the leader of the company believes are what will make the business most successful or accomplish the goals it has. Each person affiliated with the business should buy into these values or else they are just wasting their time and yours. By developing a set of values and goals and passing them on to people who agree with those values and goals, you essentially duplicate yourself every time you bring someone into your organization. Please understand that I do not expect you to have carbon copies of yourself helping you with your business. This would actually be counter productive because there would be no new ideas and conflict would be inevitable. What I am saying is that as long as the people you incorporate into your life and your business believe in the same goals you do and acceptable ways of reaching these goals, then you have essentially multiplied yourself. The greatest thing about multiplying yourself is that, because we all have our own talents, you have duplicated yourself with someone with a different skill set from yours and different insight. Each of us usually likes to do what we are best at. Some people are good at public speaking and love to do it while others would much rather build the presentation for the speaker to use because that is what they are good at. If these two people both have the same goal for the company success, and both do what they are good at, then instead of one person giving a great speech in front of a mediocre presentation or having a great presentation behind a speaker that can't get the words out right, you have a great speaker giving a great speech in front of a great presentation. You've not only duplicated yourself but improved on the original!

In my business I have surrounded myself with women who all share the goal of enriching women's lives around the world. Not only do we share the same goal, we share the same values of how to reach that goal. We believe that by leading with love and integrity and teaching everyone that wants to come along everything we know and the values that Mary Kay taught us, we are not only duplicating ourselves but we are duplicating

Mary Kay herself. By utilizing our different strengths and working together, we can all be successful and grow as a team. After all, team means: **T**ogether **E**ach **A**ccomplishes **M**ore.

Jack Welch, the legendary CEO of General Electric, which according to Bloomberg Financial is one of the largest companies in the world said, "My main job was developing talent. I was a gardener providing water and other nourishment to our top 750 people. Of course, I had to pull out some weeds, too." There are times in our careers when some people in your organization may decide to shortcut the ethics side of your business in lieu of what they may see as a more streamlined approach; they may believe that abiding by your ethics and standards is a big waste of their time. Then it is your duty to all the leaders who are following in your footsteps and doing things the right way and holding themselves to a high ethical and moral standard, to "pull those weeds." You have to be tough with people who are not behaving ethically or you jeopardize your entire organization. If people shortcut the culture and have temporary success then a certain segment is sure to follow them. Then instead of having one weed to pull, you have a bushel full. It also disheartens those who are doing things the "right" way because the spotlight is being taken off them and shining on the "shortcutters." Once there is division in the ranks, your organization can have a difficult time recovering.

A very important side note: different is not always wrong. The one thing you should cherish in your organization is diversity—diversity of cultures, ideas, styles, and thinking. You may be faced with situations in your business when someone comes along and goes about doing what you ask them to do in a completely different way and does it with resounding success! First impressions are usually skeptical when a "hot-shot" comes on the team. People automatically think that the new person is somehow bypassing the system in order to succeed rapidly, and thereby hurting the organization. But that is like saying Henry Ford, who invented the assembly line style of manufacturing, was hurting the automotive industry when he discovered a faster, more efficient way to make a car! You have to look closely at what people are doing to see if they are compromising the values and the culture of the Company or if they have just improved the organization. If the latter is true, then you have done what you set out to do and multiplied yourself. Now you'll just want to bring everyone else on board to the improvements to the system. Everyone wins. If the new system does not uphold the values and ethics of the culture then it must be removed, even if proving to be profitable. The temptation might be to compromise the values to conform to the new system for increased profits, but companies with no morals that only chase profits are doomed to fail—the people who came on board because of the values of the culture will probably leave and the people that replace them, who do not have to buy in to the values of the culture, are probably not the kind of people who care about the long term success of the business. People do not want to do business with unethical companies. The word spreads fast then there is nothing left.

Building Leaders from Within

It is easy to tell people to duplicate themselves; many times it is hard to figure out where to start. Start from within. The best way I have found to get answers is to ask the right questions. When I am looking for leadership qualities, these are the questions I ask:

* What am I looking for in a leader?

* Who are my consistent achievers?

* Who has shown resilience and "bounce back-ability"?

* Who has shown accountability for their actions?

* Who supports their leader?

* Who gets excited about doing a good job and wants more responsibility?

* Who shows belief in the company and what we are accomplishing?

* Who shows belief and support for those around them?

* Who shows a spirit of excellence?

* Who has built valuable relationships in their current role?

* Who has shown coach-ability and the desire to learn?

* Who has the values and morals I want in a leader in my organization and displays them?

As a leader you want to know your role. You want to give people guidance and clear vision of what they are to do and how they can track their progress. A leader must be bold and yet humble enough to understand that it is his or her responsibility to get along with people. Bosses try to force people to accept them; managers try to force people to accept the system; but leaders endear themselves to their people, mentor them, and show them the way. Leaders invest themselves in people with their time, respect, caring, love, and understanding. Leaders know the people in the organization's mission, why they are doing what they do, their vision, how they are going to accomplish the mission, and what they are willing to invest. Leaders remind people of their dreams, missions, and visions when they lose sight of what those might be. Leaders develop relationships based on respect and confidence. Leaders give praise for a job well done and not just a criticism for an opportunity missed. Leaders follow up on people to support their progress, always offering coaching and helping them build their skills. Most of all leaders lead by example. Mary Kay Ash would say, "A leader is someone who knows where she is going and is able to take others with her." Who will you take with you?

The Speed of the Leader

If I heard it once, I have heard it a hundred times: "The speed of the leader is the speed of the gang." Mary Kay Ash instilled this motto in us at every opportunity and I know it to be true. As a matter of fact, if I have said it once I have also said it a hundred times to myself. To be a leader means to set the pace of those you expect to follow you. Mary Kay Ash set a pace of a daring thinker and a visionary and I was part of her "gang." As a result I have always been a big thinker, and I would like to think I am a visionary as well. Mary Kay Ash taught us that hard work and leadership are rewarded; she not only taught us, she showed us through her diligent work ethic and tireless leadership. She set a pace for us to follow and it has brought me through milestones that were just dreams when I joined her "gang."

Have you ever gone into any store or business and seen the manager goofing off? I have. What I have noticed when I go into stores where the manager is loafing or unprofessional is that most of the employees are following the manager's cue. When the manager sends out the signal that working diligently and taking pride as an employee is not a priority then that signal is picked up by most of the staff. That is when I have noticed the worst customer service, the most disorderly stores, and the most apathy towards the customer. On the contrary, when you enter any business and you see the manager or supervisor sharply dressed and working diligently, helping out wherever he or she appears needed—that is when

I notice every employee striving to do a good job. As a leader the people you surround yourself with are a reflection of you. This not only means that when they mess up you look bad. It means that whatever image you project, for the most part, they will emulate. If as a leader you pay close attention to the way you dress, the way you treat and speak to those around you, the ethics you exude, and the way you work, you will lead a group that does as well. People are not sheep. They generally will not follow a bad example. But people have an uncanny knack for rising to meet the expectations laid out for them. If you set the bar low, you will get low achievement. If you set the bar high then you can expect a lot more. If you set the bar out of sight then you will have people reaching amazing heights—whether they clear the bar or not, the results will be stellar and everyone will feel a sense of accomplishment.

Roger Bannister was a child of poor parents who grew up in England in the 1940s and 50s. Roger desperately wanted to go to college to study medicine but he knew his parents would never be able to afford to send him to a university, let alone medical school. So Roger decided if he wanted to be a doctor, he would have to earn a scholarship. Being a naturally good runner, Roger focused his efforts and worked hard to hone his skills both as a runner and student. His hard work paid off and he was granted a track scholarship to one of the most prestigious universities in the world, Oxford University. He continued to train and won a lot of events and a lot of attention from the press. After finishing a disappointing fourth in the 1500 meter race in the 1952 Olympic Games, the media—who had previously praised him—turned on him and said he needed better coaching and training methods. As a result his focus changed. He devoted himself to his medical studies and trained as a runner just forty-five minutes a day. But his goal was clear. And on May 6, 1954, after a morning of terrible weather on a muddy track, Roger Bannister became a full-time medical student who was the first person to run a mile in less than four minutes in the history of track competition.

He astonished the world with his feat and his feet. Although he is the one who received the lion's share of the glory and eventually knighthood, Roger Bannister did not accomplish on his own what many people thought to be an impossible task. Two teammates, Chris Brasher and Christopher Chataway, paced him. During training and races one would start the race at a blistering pace, forcing Bannister to get off to a fast start while following his teammate. In the meantime, the other lagged a bit behind. Then toward the end of the race the teammate, who had been conserving his energy, would speed up his pace and relieve the other pacer while Bannister never lost a step. At the end of the race, the second pacer would fall off, allowing Bannister to sprint to the finish. Even though Roger Bannister was the one who received practically immortal fame and glory for his record, this training technique led all three runners to fantastic athletic accomplishments. Chris Brasher won an Olympic gold medal in the 1956 Sydney Olympic Games in the 3,000-meter steeplechase while Christopher Chataway set his own world record in the 5,000-meter race at the London versus Moscow athletic competition in 1954. In this example it is difficult to say who the leader was and who "the gang" was, but what is certain is that they set a blistering pace that they all used to achieve greatness.

As a leader I see it as my place to set the pace for the people I work with. I have never sat back and relied on the work done in the past to carry me through while I took a break. That would not be fair to those who look to me as a leader and an inspiration. Although I work differently than someone just starting out in this business, I am sure it is obvious that I was always working to make my area the best. I have always tried to help people dream bigger dreams. I see the potential in people and I always believe in them, even when they don't always believe in themselves. As a result, I have to be a big thinker. I have to set a brisk pace for people to follow in hopes that, for some, I will be the pacer and they will be the record breaker. So many people are conditioned to think that greatness only happens to other people. I do my best to help everyone realize that greatness can happen to them; as a result I work to get them to think as big as I do. Then I hope they think bigger. No matter what career any of the people I deal with end up pursuing, I hope it is a dream bigger than they ever dared to dream before. I hope that, by setting a pace and dreaming big, everyone who has ever been a part of my "gang" strives to break records long after I have left the stadium.

Whenever I think of who "my gang" has been over the years, I have to thank Linda McBroom, Johnnette Shealy, Karlee Isenhart, and Shirley Oppenheimer—all who have run with me and paced me. Together we have run a race that has spanned thirty years and have seen miracles happen.

Your Attitude Determines Your Altitude

The single most important lesson I have learned in my Mary Kay business is the importance of a positive attitude. You see, I was not the most positive person when I began my Mary Kay business in 1975. I had grown up in a very loving and caring household, but my parents were never very positive people. If you asked them they would probably tell you they lived in the "real world" where the husband would work hard at whatever job he had been lucky enough to get because of a trade he was fortunate enough to learn, while his wife would stay at home and take care of the children and the house. Dreaming of better things and talking about positive things was for dreamers and there never seemed to be much room for dreamers in the "real world." In the "real world" things just were what they were and you accepted them as real life; your attitude was a reflection of the struggles of daily life. But Mary Kay Ash told us all that our attitude would determine our altitude. In other words, if you believe you can, then you can—and if you believe you can't then you are probably right too.

Well, that was completely against everything I had learned in the "real world." I was taught to grumble about the weather when it rained then complain about the heat when the sun came out. I was taught that our lives were a product of everything that happened around us and that it was pretty much out of our control. But here was this lady who told me that all I had to do was believe that positive things were coming my way, and whatever I wanted to do or be was up to me. It was like a revelation! I took that advice to heart and began to do everything I could to be a positive person. Amazing things started to happen; my business began to grow, my husband started thinking more positively, and both of my children realized that there was nothing they couldn't do if they set their minds to it. We moved out of the "real world" and into a world where anything good was possible. I guess other people noticed it too because as a brand new Independent Sales Director I was invited to speak at a Sales Director's debut in St. Louis, Missouri. I was in a group of Sales Directors chit chatting and the conversation became—how should I put it?—less than positive, so I left. As I walked away I heard a lady in the group sneer, "You can't talk negative in front of Pat, she won't listen." I have to admit, I was hurt at the time that they would say that like there was something wrong with me, but now I see it as a compliment. I choose to surround myself with positive people and I distance myself from negative people. Positive people give me energy and negative people seem to drain it right out of me, so I choose not to be around negativity. I believe that winners attract winners and misery loves company ... so I will stick with the winners and avoid the misery as much as possible.

A dear friend of mine, Brian Robertson, exemplified one of my favorite Mary Kay quotes. Brian, who was an avid golfer, was practicing at the driving range and got so exhausted that he couldn't finish his practice. He went home and took a shower and noticed that the water beating on his arms was actually leaving marks! He was not feeling well and decided that there may be something wrong with him. He asked his wife Carol, who was then an Independent Executive Senior Sales Director, to take him to the hospital. After an examination and a few tests, he was immediately admitted to the hospital. As they sat in his room, Brian and Carol were joined by a doctor who gave them the devastating news that he had been diagnosed with stage-three leukemia. Of course they were upset but they were not defeated. Carol and Brian had always been some of the most wonderfully positive people I had ever been around. It was always a joy and a pleasure to be with the Robertson's and their family because they were beaming with gracious hearts and positive thinking. They discussed his treatment options and Brian made a conscious decision about his attitude even at such a trying time. That day Brian took a marker and on the dry erase board in his room, he wrote in bold letters, "What the mind can conceive and the heart truly believes, you can achieve. The fight begins today." He had taken a quote we had heard Mary Kay say so many times and he exemplified what it meant to have a positive attitude. At every turn during his treatment, we were told that the chances of his survival were slim. People told us that he wouldn't make it through the treatments, but we didn't listen. Then we heard that even if he did make it through the treatments he would probably get sick because his immune system was so weak, but we didn't listen and just kept everything positive about his situation. In spite of all of the naysayers and realists, six months later Brian was playing golf with my husband while Carol and I walked on the beach; the cancer was in remission and we all celebrated New Years together. Brian was back with his usual laughter and country boy charm, untarnished by the trials he had been through, and Carol's beaming smile never seemed more brilliant. They never let negativity creep into their lives. Ultimately, Brian lost his battle with cancer, but he lived long enough to see his wife become an Independent National Sales Director, his daughter blossom from a baby into an adorable little girl, and his stepdaughter get married. We know that even though cancer took his life in the end, it never dampened his spirit and his positive attitude.

The day before Brian passed away my son-in-law, Chad, went to see him in his hospital room. Chad walked in and Brian greeted him with a warm smile and a, "Hey, brother!" When Chad asked him how he was feeling Brian told him that his legs hurt a little and the doctors were going to give him something for it, but once that was taken care of they were going to send him home. Chad left their visit feeling great that his friend was back on the road to recovery and that Brian was as optimistic as ever. Chad ran into Carol in the hallway as she was rushing in frantically to see Brian. She stopped in the hallway and she asked Chad how Brian was doing. Chad told her he was fine and was looking forward to going home. What Chad didn't know was that Brain's condition had worsened, but Brian would not give up his fight and his positive attitude. Carol told Chad later that she knew Brian wasn't as good as he led Chad to believe, but it gave her a chance to check her attitude before she went in to see him. If Brian wasn't giving up then neither would she.

Some of the most positive people I have ever had the pleasure of working with are the men and women of the Philippines. My daughter Pam and I have been traveling to the Philippines since the Mary Kay subsidiary opened for business there in 1999, and have made a lot of really great friends there. If you have never been to the Philippines, there are two things I can tell you. It is hot—really hot—and when it rains, *it rains!* But even as positive as Pam and I are, when we saw the monsoon rains pouring down outside of our hotel just before we were going to have one of our first guest events in the Philippines, we became a little disheartened. We were sure that nobody would come out to a Mary Kay guest event in a torrential downpour. The streets looked like rivers and you could hardly see down the block through the driving rain. But one by one the room filled to capacity and then to overflowing! I turned to one of the Filipino women I had befriended and said, "Can you believe this rain?" She replied, "I know, blessings are chasing us down." I learned a valuable lesson from that woman. It's all a matter of perspective. You see without the rain we couldn't have food, flowers, or fresh water to drink; without it we couldn't live. When you put it in perspective, getting wet seems like a minor inconvenience.

I believe we make a choice every morning when we wake up. We can be positive or we can be negative. We can be happy or we can be in a bad mood, and it can happen so fast! Have you ever heard the expression, "You must have gotten up on the wrong side of the bed this morning"? Well that is because people who don't think about and choose their attitude let their attitude choose them. They let their circumstances of the first few minutes they are awake determine their attitude for the rest of the day. It seems ridiculous to me that we can let getting a run in your stockings or a broken shoelace determine how you look at those around you and the whole world. I take a few minutes every morning before I even get out of bed and smile. The funny thing about smiling is if something makes you happy, you smile; but if you smile when nothing is happening, it makes you happy! What a wonderful gift God has given us to adjust our mood. By simply turning the corners of your mouth up you can get yourself in a good mood.

Once I'm in a good mood I think of the wonderful things in my life that I am happy for—my children, my husband, my grandchildren, and my wonderful life. Now I am filled with not only happiness but a sense of gratitude. The best thing about it is that it only takes a couple of minutes. You won't make yourself late for anything, but you can be a happier person all day. When you start your day with happiness and gratitude you realize that maybe those stockings were ready for the trash anyway or those shoes would look so much better with new laces. It is much easier to find the good in situations when you realize all the blessings you already have in your life. When you make a conscious decision to be in a good mood and to have a positive outlook on life then the great things that happen are that much more appreciated, and the challenges we encounter don't seem as daunting.

Once you have made the decision to be positive you need to constantly monitor the things you say aloud and to yourself. What you think about you talk about. What you talk about you bring about. So if you go around thinking, *I'm not that good at talking in front of a group, I get too nervous,* you are actually telling your brain, *We are not good at talking in front of groups, be prepared—if there is a group do not talk well in front of them, get nervous.* Then the next time you have to address a group your subconscious rifles through its files of what to do and what do those files say?

* Get nervous

* Sweat

* Dry out mouth

* Forget key points

* Panic

Then when you flounder through your speech and sit down your brain says, *Good job everyone, we don't speak well in front of groups. Mission accomplished.* I would prefer that you tell yourself, *I am an excellent speaker and speaking in front of a group is fun and easy.* Give your subconscious some positive files to flip through. Then when you speak in front of a group, even if you stumble you can recover easier, smile, and finish because speaking in front of a group is fun and easy. Muhammad Ali once said, "It's the repetition of affirmations that leads to belief. And once that belief becomes a deep conviction, things begin to happen." If you will remember, when Muhammad Ali was still a struggling boxer named Cassius Clay, he would boldly tell interviewers, "I am the greatest boxer of all time!" He told anyone who would listen how great he was. Of course he had yet to prove that he was the greatest boxer of all time because he had not yet proven himself in the boxing ring. Many people thought he was an arrogant braggart. It is true that he had a lot of self-confidence; but, as it turns out, was not saying the things he was saying for our benefit as much as he was saying them as affirmations to himself. He was a consummate showman, but beneath all of the theatrics was a man who was constantly affirming to himself that he was the greatest boxer of all time. Now he is known as one of the greatest, if not *the* greatest, boxer of all time.

Similarly to Mary Kay, Henry Ford said, "If you think you can do a thing or if you think you can't do a thing, you're right." To illustrate this point I tell a story from time to time that my son brought back from basketball camp one year. The story is about a young and talented basketball player named Dunk McDunk. Dunk McDunk was playing so well in high school that he started getting noticed by some of the premier colleges in the country. As a result the colleges all began to send scouts to see this young basketball star. The scouts all said they loved his talent but were just a little worried that he wouldn't be tall enough to compete at the college level because he was only five feet eight inches tall. One scout mentioned that if he could dunk the basketball, all the concern would go away and he would certainly be invited to play at the school of his choice, but if he couldn't dunk the basketball then he may not get a scholarship. Word soon got around that the best coaches in the country from the very best schools were all going to come to the next game to see how he performed. Dunk McDunk knew he had to dunk the basketball during the game to impress the visiting coaches. To this end, every day after practice he would stay late and try to dunk the ball and every day he would come up just a little short. No matter what he tried he could not dunk the ball. *The goal was just too high,* he thought. Finally, Thursday night before the game he had an idea. He was barely missing the goal, so if he could just lower the goals one inch he should be able to dunk. So he lowered the goals and began to practice. Sure enough he could dunk the ball. Before long he could dunk it forwards or backwards with one hand or two. He was putting on quite a display on the lowered goals. Satisfied he went home for the night.

The next evening in the game his opportunity came. He stole the ball from an opposing player and dribbled as fast as he could down the court, leaped into the air, and performed an amazing dunk that impressed the coaches and sent a thunderous cheer through the crowd. After the game the coaches all wanted to talk to Dunk McDunk to see when he would like to tour their respective campuses. Dunk spoke to them all but in the back of his mind he felt terrible. After the gym cleared he made his way to his trusted coach's office. "Coach," he said. "I need to talk to you."

"What's on your mind, Dunk?" asked the coach.

"Last night, I lowered the goals so I could dunk the ball, now I feel like I have been dishonest to all the fans and the college coaches. How should I tell them?" asked Dunk McDunk.

The coach smiled and replied, "I lock up the gym every night. I saw you lower the goals to practice. So when you left, I raised them back up again."

If you think you can, you can. If you think you can't you're probably right too.

> *If you think you can you can. If you think you can't you're probably right too.*

Sometimes it is not as easy to remember to be positive and negative things slip out. That's when it's time for reinforcements. What I have done and encouraged others to do is to wear a rubber band around your wrist and whenever you catch yourself saying something like, "I never get parking spaces up front," stretch the rubber band out and give yourself a little snap. Don't hurt yourself; it is just a reminder to say, "There are always open spaces up front when I need one." You will be amazed how those spaces will just start appearing for you. I get tickled when I ride with my daughter and my beautiful grandchildren, Jacob and Katie, are in the car. Pam is one of the most positive people I know and she is constantly passing it on to her children. We always seem to get great parking spaces and Pam will say, "Rock star parking, right up front." The kids respond, "We always get a great parking spot; you're a parking shark, Mommy." As long as they've been riding together, especially when Jacob and Katie were still in strollers, they have always heard their mother's positive affirmation that she always gets a great parking spot because she is a parking shark. They may not call them positive affirmations, but they know to say, "I love math, I'm great at math and math is fun and easy." Because they know that, "I can't do it," or, "I'm terrible at math," will be met with a strong rebuke from my daughter or son-in-law.

Of course, just because you say, "I never get speeding tickets," doesn't mean you can drive eighty miles per hour in a school zone and be invisible to the police. But when you are constantly telling yourself how easy tasks are that seem to be more difficult for you and how favorable things are always happening to you, I think you will be amazed at the changes you will see. Then one day you will begin to notice how miserable it must be when you hear the constant grumbling of the negative people around you and when you hear someone at a table next to you say, "The kitchen never cooks my food right," or, "With my luck, I'll miss my train and be late for work." You will think to yourself, *What you think about, you bring about.*

I remember when my grandson Jacob was born. He had been out of the hospital for a month and weighed only an ounce more than when he was born, and he had a little cough. My daughter had taken him to the doctor several times and they told her it was nothing—he probably just needed to eat more often and probably had some dried milk in his throat. Finally, she had heard him cough long enough and she took him back to the doctor and got an X-ray of his chest. The doctor told Pam to get Jacob to the hospital right away; he had full-blown pneumonia. As my tiny grandbaby lay in the hospital we rushed to Virginia to be with him. We were there when the doctors finally diagnosed him with Cystic Fibrosis. Soon after we got a call from Mary Kay's assistant, Erma Thompson, then Mary Kay picked up the phone to check on us and let us know that she was concerned. She talked to me first and asked me how I was. I couldn't quite muster my customary, "I'm great," so I said, "I'm fine; we're all fine just a little sad today."

After a short conversation, Mary Kay spoke to Pam and when she got off the phone, my daughter looked at me and told me quite frankly, "Jacob is doing better now that we know what was wrong with him and we are not sad." I realized that day that the lesson Mary Kay had taught me had come full circle. She taught it to me, I taught it to Pam and, when I needed it the most, she taught it back to me. There is no day so dark as the day you lose hope. Once having a positive attitude becomes a way of life for you, you will never have to fear that bleak day.

I surround myself with only positive people and negativity is like a germ to me. Because these many years later that one comment still rings true. "You can't talk negative around Pat Fortenberry, she won't listen to it."

School Is Never Out for the Pro

Since the first day of my Mary Kay business, I have been a sponge for information. I have listened to tapes and CDs of top Sales Directors, National Sales Directors, motivational speakers, and sales experts. I have listened to and read every word I could get my hands on from Mary Kay Ash herself and done anything I could to get face to face with her. I had never been a sales person before I began my Mary Kay business. I had been a social worker, a Home Economist, and a home-maker. I started my business with a showcase and a pocketful of enthusiasm but not much else. I didn't know how to sell. So I decided if this was going to be my new life that I had better learn. I guess it has worked because I'm still here after more than thirty years. But I am still a sponge. I still read books on leadership, attitude, and motivation. One of my favorite authors and speakers, John Maxwell, has retreats with a small group every year and a few years ago I went, even though my working life was winding down, because I knew I would learn something from him that could make me a better leader and a better person. At that retreat I had the honor of hearing from Mrs. Corretta Scott King, wife of civil rights pioneer Martin Luther King, Jr., before she passed away. I was able to hear firsthand from the wife personal stories of the life of, in my opinion, one of the most fearless and influential leaders the world has ever known. She told us that Dr. King was never too busy to help a friend in need and that he truly held in his heart unconditional love for everyone he met. Her message really struck a cord for me. Her message reinforced my belief that when you lead with unconditional love, you can overcome any obstacle and reach any goal. The personal time I was able to spend with Mrs. King, learning from her was certainly a highlight of my life. I firmly believe that learning is a journey not a destination.

I'm sure you have heard the expression *dumb enough to listen but smart enough to follow through.* I don't think that saying is very positive, but I do agree that everyone can be *humble* enough to listen and *diligent* enough to follow through. We are never too good to learn from someone else. I constantly find inspiration and wonderful ideas from brand new Independent Beauty Consultants and Independent Sales Directors. I would never presume that because someone does not have the longevity in the business that I have that they have nothing to bring to the table. A dear friend and offspring Independent National Sales Director, Kimberly Copeland, began her Mary Kay business in her early twenties and became the youngest ever to reach the position of Independent National Sales

Director when she debuted. She began with more than just a pretty smile and a cheerleader's spirit. She shook up the way we did the business from the ground up. She broke belief barriers about how fast we could move up the career path in our company, how hard we could work, and what we could expect from less experienced Consultants and Sales Directors. It would have been easy to doubt Kimberly in the beginning because we have always heard that if something or someone seems too good to be true then it or they probably are. Well that only works until the paradigm shifts.

A paradigm is a set of values or assumptions that determines how you view your reality. A paradigm shift is when someone or something comes along and changes those assumptions and changes the way you view reality. For example, for thousands of years just about everyone had learned and was convinced that the earth was the center of the universe and that the sun, moon, and stars all revolved around the stationary and all-important earth. It made sense. If you look at the sun it seems to rise and set. The moon follows the same pattern at night and the stars are never in the same place night after night, and it certainly doesn't seem like the earth is moving at all. But in the 15th century, Nicolaus Copernicus—a mathematician, astrologer, physician, and all-around scholar—decided that earth was not the stationary center of the universe, but it just seems that way because of what we have been taught. He explained his theory in *Nicholas Copernicus On the Revolutions,* translation and commentary by Edward Rosen.

For when a ship is floating calmly along, the sailors see its motion mirrored in everything outside, while on the other hand they suppose that they are stationary, together with everything on board. In the same way, the motion of the earth can unquestionably produce the impression that the entire universe is rotating.

He proposed though that the earth along with the other planets was circling around the sun and spinning at the same time. His theories caused quite a stir at the time and he and his theories were actually rejected by the Church for hundreds of years. Galileo was actually forced by the Church to denounce Copernicus and his theories and plead to be imprisoned for life, rather than executed, almost a century after Copernicus first revealed his theories! One of the greatest thinkers of all time was imprisoned for the rest of his life because he supported the fact that the earth revolves around the sun, a fact that we learn as children today.

Of course the story of Copernicus is a dramatic example of how someone can come along and change our paradigms and our view of what is possible and what is not. In business we have to realize that we can constantly learn from those around us and create new realities of what is possible. In my area that paradigm shift came from Kimberly. For two decades we assumed that it took about ten years to become an Independent National Sales Director. Some did it a little sooner and most took much longer to make it to that position. But Kimberly began her Mary Kay business and after debuting as a Sales Director in December of 2000 it took her exactly three years until she became an Independent National Sales Director, debuting in December of 2003. Through her hard work, determination, and unbending focus on her goal, Kimberly created a paradigm shift for thousands of women who watched her accomplish what we all thought was impossible. By watching her we all learned that we still had a lot to learn about the business' possibilities. Although I had been an Independent National Sales Director for nineteen years, I learned from this young woman, that everything I knew was just the tip of the iceberg of what there is to know about the business. I soaked it up like a sponge once again.

Even though I am no longer an active Independent Sales Force Member, I still strive to learn something everyday. I am still a leader and through my faith I am still led; I teach myself each day how to be a little better at being both. I still read books and watch DVDs on the latest concepts of leadership and self-improvement because I can always be better tomorrow than I am today. As long as people will listen to me I will pass on what I have learned from all of my experiences so that others can build on the foundation I have laid. I have not always been right and I will still make mistakes, but I have always learned from the mistakes I have made and will strive to learn for the ones not yet made. To stop thirsting for knowledge is to accept a life fulfilled and that there is nothing left to know. I fear death would follow soon after such a revelation, so I choose to never be content with what I know. I choose to never be fulfilled with having learned enough. Grandma Moses didn't start painting until she was in her seventies. She became a world-renowned artist in her lifetime and traveled the galleries of the world exhibiting her work. What if she had decided that she had nothing else to learn or teach? I have heard the old wives' tale that every time you learn something you get another wrinkle in your brain; if that is the case then that is the only place on my body that I will gladly accept and welcome as many wrinkles as I can get. Since I believe that school is never out for the pro, all I can say is wrinkle on brain, wrinkle on!

Know Thyself

To know thyself means to know everything about yourself. Not just the good things, not just the bad things, not how you think you are, but how and what you truly are. This seems like an easy task to handle; after all you have been living with yourself longer than anyone. But in actuality, to truly know yourself can be one of the hardest, most painful, and yet enlightening things you can ever do. The sad part is that we spend our whole lives getting to know our partners or our friends; sometimes we can really put them under a microscope and pick out every flaw, bad habit, or imperfection in them—but we never tend to turn the interrogation light on ourselves.

"But what good can possibly come out of picking out my flaws?" you may ask. To know yourself is not to pick out your flaws. However, you may learn some things about yourself that you had developed into habits, and may find some areas of improvement that you would want to work on—but the goal is to know your true strengths and weaknesses. John Maxwell taught me to rate strengths from 1 to 10, with a 1 being much more of a weakness than a strength, and a 10 being a great strength. Then pick the things to work on. You would think that you should take everything that is the lowest and work diligently to raise those scores. I thought I would pick the 2s, 3s, and 4s. Certainly I don't want to have weaknesses! I want to be as close to perfect as I can! How realistic is that? He taught me that with a tremendous amount of effort, you can probably raise your score three points maximum. That's all—three points. So his philosophy is, why waste all your time and energy working to go from poor to mediocre? Why spend energy to raise your score from a 2 to a 5? That's just average; that's not a strength, that is what lots of people have. Instead, Mr. Maxwell taught me to take the 7s, 8s, and 9s and turn those into 10s! What a revolutionary idea.

Instead of nit picking attributes of our personalities that aren't as strong as they could be, work with what we are good at. After all, we are never going to be perfect. No matter how hard we work, no matter what we do, we are not going to be perfect. Not in this lifetime anyway. So what is the point of spinning your wheels trying to have straight 10s across the board? If you focus energy on your strengths then you can use them to take you anywhere you want to go. And the great thing is that when you realize what your weaknesses are, you can surround yourself with people who are good at those things to help you out. If you must know, I would not consider myself a good organizer. When it comes to being organized I am probably a 3, but when it comes to working with people I am about as close to a 10 as anyone. I could work and work and work to keep things in their right place, and work on filing my receipts and keeping promotional material where I can get to it easily, but if I spend night and day striving to get more organized I would probably be able to get it right about half of the time. That would make me a 5 or a 6. But all that time I spend organizing, what am I not doing? I'm not working with people! Thank goodness there is a solution that I learned long before John Maxwell taught it to me. I hired people who are 10s at being organized. My secretary Galinda is my "in case of emergency break glass" person. I can count on her to be able to find whatever it is I need out of thirty years of accumulated stuff. She can pull up a flyer we made five yeas ago in about thirty seconds, have it updated, printed out, and on my desk in two minutes. I don't know where in the world I would be if it was not for Galinda, but I can be sure it would have been a bumpy road to where ever it was. I also have Charles. The United States Air Force "motivated" him to be organized and it has paid off for me in my business and in life. The fact that he is organized is not why I married him; we could have always hired a bookkeeper, but it is one of his strengths. He can take the receipts and make sure they are filed, pay all of the bills on time, and keep track of our finances with the best of them. It a strength of his and we rely on it and I am grateful for it.

So what to do now, right? Take out a sheet of paper and write down all of the attributes that you think you would need to be successful. Do you need to be able to work well with others? Do you need to be able to speak well in front of a group? Do you need to be organized or a good speller or coordinated? Then rate your proficiency at each attribute. Be honest with yourself. Then look at your list and focus on the strengths and look for help with the ones that might never get that high. If your goal is to build a house and you know that you can coordinate colors and decorate better than Martha Stewart, but you can't hit a nail on the head if your life depended on it, you may want to surround yourself with a few carpenters. Let them drive the nails while you enhance your skills on the latest decorating ideas and techniques. Work with your strengths and delegate your weaknesses and you can be successful in anything you want to do.

Another way to know yourself is to take a personality test. There are tons of them out there. You can find them online or you can probably find someone in your community that can administer one. The one I have used for years is the DISC test. The test will place you in a category according to how you score based on four personality traits. These traits are:

Dominance: D's are strong-willed and strong-minded. They like challenges, they take action, and they expect immediate results.

Influence: I's are optimistic and extroverted. They like participating on teams, sharing ideas, and energizing and entertaining others.

Steadiness: S's are sympathetic and cooperative. They are helpful people who like working behind the scenes, performing in consistent and predictable ways, and being good listeners.

Conscientiousness: C's are concerned and correct. They are sticklers for quality and like planning ahead, employing systematic approaches, and checking and re-checking for accuracy.

Many people find that they may think they would be categorized as one category, but the test (and usually their friends thereafter) will show them they are actually something completely different. For example, many people may think they are an S, just attempting to help out the group, but the test will show them to be a D. If you ask anyone who works on projects with that person they will almost always tell you that person is definitely a D. Then reading the profile, the person will usually agree with everything it says then they realize they are a D. That is what I mean by know thyself. We oftentimes think of ourselves one way, the way we would like to be or the way we used to be, and that is still the perception we have of ourselves. Perhaps the person in our example grew up in a house with a mother that was a very high D. In order to get along the daughter may have acted more like an S in the home. But as she grew up and got out in the world on her own she may act more and more like her mother, a high D, but still thinks she is an S.

The great thing about knowing your personality, and none is better or worse than the other, is that analysis can also teach you how to recognize the personality traits of others and in turn the best ways to interact with him or her. Once you realize the different traits you will realize that if you are dealing with a C personality, pressing them for a spontaneous decision or an immediate answer to a proposal will not get you anywhere. A C personality will want to check your facts and crunch the numbers and read the fine print before making a decision, maybe two or three times! If you realize that you are dealing with a C personality, you will know to present all of the facts very thoroughly and not be upset if they double-check everything you say. It's not that they don't trust you; it is just in their nature. Likewise, if you know you are a D personality, then you will know that the reason you are feeling a little frustrated is because you like immediate action. You will also realize that if you want to do business with a C personality you will need to find some patience. Just by knowing this about yourself, you can diffuse a situation in your head by thinking, *Oh, this person is just a C personality, it's not that they don't like what I had to say or don't trust me. This is just going to take some time, so I might as well relax.* I have found that over the years, learning the different personality traits has helped me work with everyone. D's want to hear how they can be in charge of their own destiny; I's want to know how much fun it can be and how many new people they can meet; S's want to know what it can do for their family and how they can help; and C's want to know all the facts and figures, but they'll get back to you later. If you can identify the personality of the person you are talking to, you can tailor what you say to what interests them the most. I'm not saying just tell them what they want to hear, but you can emphasize the points that are most likely to interest them. If you know the common stumbling blocks that can occur between your personality type and theirs, you can be extra careful to tone down those aspects of your personality so you can communicate without your D's or S's or I's or C's getting in the way.

Raise Your Deserve Level

Mary Kay used to always tell us, "God has never made a nobody, only somebodies." Truer words have never been spoken. There is no difference between you and the Queen of England or the King of Denmark or any other successful person in this whole world. The fact that the Queen of England or the King of Denmark were born into royal families doesn't make them any different from you or me, it just happened by chance. But at the basic level they are just a man and a woman; they are the same as we are but they have one thing most people don't have. They have the belief that they deserve to be a queen and a king. They have been taught from a very young age that it is their right and privilege to rule their countries. They have been taught that they deserve the trappings of their position and the responsibilities that go with them. They are not geniuses or keepers of some wisdom that makes them more capable than most other people; they are just like you and me. Because this is the case, it makes me so sad when I meet people who are holding themselves back from chasing a dream or excelling in business when they have the skills; it is often in their power to be or to do anything they want,. They have been trained that success, wealth, and privilege belong to others, not them. I hear people all the time that tell me they are happy with the way things are in their life; but after talking to them for a while I hear that they don't really like their job, or they wish their kids could go to private school, or they think it must be nice to be able to go on fancy trips. When I hear these things and things like it, I know I am talking to someone who has been trained to think that they don't deserve success. Surely no one has ever sat them down and told them, "You don't deserve a wonderful life so don't expect one." What I mean is that over time the people around that person have conditioned him or her to believe that being successful is like being royalty or winning the lottery. It only happens to a few other people, so be happy with what you've got. Well, I'm here to tell you that that is ridiculous. God has planted the seeds of greatness in each and every one of us and it is our duty to nurture that seed, help it grow, and see what it becomes.

One of the most recognizable, famous, and greatest athletes in recent history, Michael Jordan, is a prime example. Michael grew up in a small house in Wilmington, North Carolina, not too far from where I live. He was not born into a "basketball family." He was not the child of elite, athletic parents. He wasn't even the best basketball player in his high school. The man who would go on to be considered "the greatest ever" in the world of basketball was cut from his junior varsity basketball squad because the coach didn't think he was good enough. But Michael Jordan believed that he deserved to be on that team. He had been taught by his parents that he could be anything he wanted to be. And he wanted to be a basketball player. He knew the seed of greatness was inside of him; it was just going to take some nurturing. After being cut from the junior varsity team he rededicated himself to practicing. He had a dirt court at his house and a rickety rim that he practiced on every morning before school and every night after school until long after dark. He was nurturing the seed of greatness within himself. Even when he was working part-time as a dishwasher at a little diner called Whitey's he knew he deserved to be a basketball player. Well, most of you know how this story turns out, Michael Jordan went on to win six NBA championships, five NBA Most Valuable Player Awards, six NBA Finals Most Valuable Player Awards, was a twelve time NBA All-Star and a Gold Medal Olympian—just to name a few of his accolades. Michael Jordan could have listened to the coach who told him he wasn't good enough, but he knew he deserved to be a basketball player. He raised his deserve level and then put in the work to make the team, then he raised his deserve level again and decided he should be able to play in the college ranks; after excelling there he raised his deserve level again and went pro.

I tell people all the time, "If it can happen to anyone it can happen to you." Of course there are people who have talents others don't have, but we all have talents that can make us great. Mother Teresa may not have had the talents to have been an NBA All-Star, but God planted the seed of greatness in her heart—the seed of compassion—and she became world renowned for the way she nurtured that seed. She did great works with her talents and believed that she deserved to be a champion of the less fortunate, that she deserved to speak to world leaders, that she could speak for the downtrodden all over the world, and that she could do the things that God called her to do. She knew she deserved the power to make a difference in the world. From a tiny, open-air school in the slums of Calcutta, India, Mother Teresa began an outreach program that has helped hundreds of thousands of people throughout the world and preaches a message of peace that won her the Nobel Peace Prize in 1979 and lives on today long after she has passed.

I believe everyone deserves to be great. I don't think that means everyone must strive for wealth or power. I believe there are women who stay in abusive relationships because they don't think they deserve kindness and love. I believe that too many people accept the life that has happened to them instead of creating the life they want, simply because some-where along the way it was programmed in their brain that they are where they deserve to be. I also believe that by raising your deserve level you communicate not only to yourself but to all of those around you that you are nurturing the seed of

If it can happen to anyone it can happen to you."

greatness inside you, and whatever that leads you to can be where you truly deserve to be.

Where would you be if no one ever told you that you could be great? I have been successful at building my Mary Kay business for more than thirty years and now that I am retired, I am still nurturing my seed of greatness. I believe I deserve the success that I have achieved—and I have worked very hard to be where I am—but I also think the greatest is still yet to come. I don't think God planted the seed of greatness in me to make a lot of money. But I do believe that he planted a seed of greatness in me to help others, and he put Mary Kay and the mission statement of enriching women's lives in my life. I believe I have done that—enriched women's lives—and will continue to make a difference as long as I have on this earth. I believe that, if through my speeches or even this book, one person can be inspired to nurture their seed of greatness—to raise their deserve level, and realize that they deserve to be happy, treated well, and successful—then I have done what God has put me here to do.

Photo Gallery

Patricia Moak Age 3

Pat's Parents: Larkin & Ruby Moak

Pat & Charles Wedding, June 29, 1963
Mt. Pleasant Baptist Church

Pat as a DIQ with Mary Kay, December, 1976

Pat Debuting as a Director with Mary Kay January 1977

Pat receiving the most cherished award in Mary Kay Annual Miss Go-Give Award, Presenting Pat the awards is Gerald Allen Vice President of Sale 1981

Pat, Charles, Pam and Craig with Mary Kay in December 1983

Pat Crowned Queen of Sales Sapphire Seminar 1984

Pat and Mary Kay at the Las Vegas Guest Night November 1985

Pat and Family

Pat, Mary Kay and Richard Rogers
25th Anniversary 1988

Brian and Carol Robertson

Our Travel Buddies Accapulco, Mexico 1993
Top row left to right:
Virginia Robirds, Pat Fortenberry, Cheryl Warfield, Emily Mclaughlin.
Bottom row:
Joanne Holman, Carolyn Ward, Sally Rattray.

Our Husbands with Mary Kay
Left to right: Larry Ward,Charles Fortenberry, Jerry Holman' Rob
Warfield, Mary Kay, Harold Robirds, Dick McLaughlin, Bill Rattray

Pat & Pam in their NSD Suits!
Pat's 1st picture with daughter Pam Fortenberry-Slate after Pam
debuts as a Indendent National Sales Director. January 2005

Family at Seminar 2005

Honoring my Personal Assistant of 22 Years Galinda Barefoot

Pat and Charles St. Tropei France 1997

Pat's Grandchildren
Jacob And Kate Ann Venditti

FORTENBERRY FAMILY NATIONAL SALES DIRECTORS

SEATING LEFT TO RIGHT: KARLEE ISENHART, LINDA McBROOM,
PAT FORTENBERRY, JOHNNETTE SHEALY, SHIRLEY OPPENHEIMER
STANDING: VICKY FUSELIER, MICHELLE SUDETH, AMY DUNLAP, KELLY McCARROLL,
PAM FORTENBERRY-SLATE, RHONDA FRACZKOWSKI, SCARLETT WALKER,
DONNA MEIXSELL, TERRI SCHAFER, GENA GASS AND KIMBERLY COPELAND

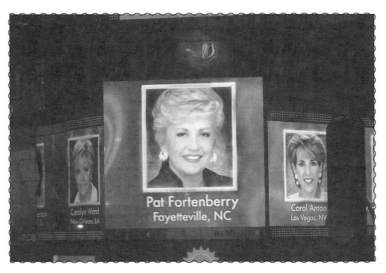

Time Square picture of Pat Fortenberry,
Inner Circle Trip May 2005

Malaysia Seminar 2005

Philippine Directors with Pat and Pam Seminar 2005

Executive Senior Directors Marita Del Corro & Maribel Dizon. They will soon be Nationals in the Philippines.

Pat with Donna Meixsell Queen of Sales Ruby Seminar 2005

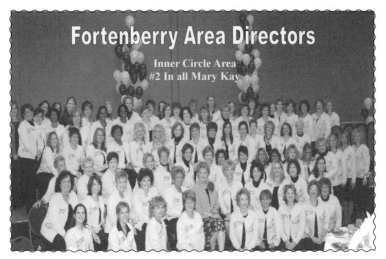

Fortenberry Inner Circle Area Directors

Family with extended Family Easter 2006

Family Seminar 2006

Pat and Charles with Tom Whatley, Vice chairman, Mary Kay Inc

Pat Receiving $9Million Plaque from President US Darrel Overcash

Pat's Family after her Retirement in San Diego, Ca. January 2007

There Is No Jury. Why Be a Judge?

God made each one of us. God also made each one of us different. He endowed each one of us with special talents and gifts. We each have unique gifts that we can contribute to each other and the world. Since that is the case, and most of us know it is the case, then why do we constantly make judgment calls about people as soon as we see them? We pre-judge almost everyone we meet. The word prejudice has become a very nasty and negative word, but the root of it means to judge before knowing—to pre-judge. But we do just that to almost everyone we meet. We can walk into a store and see people come out, and think, "He looks mean," or "She seems nice," when in reality we haven't met them at all. The guy who "looks mean" may be a revered philanthropist who jut got some bad news on a phone call and was upset, or the woman who "seems nice" could be a shoplifter who was making her escape and was happy the alarms didn't go off as she walked out the door. Of course these are extreme examples; but what I see every day is people that pre-judge others' abilities by the way they look or talk, and discount or expect less of them without giving them a chance.

Kim Caveretta is a dear friend of mine and a wonderful Mary Kay Independent Sales Director. She has been very successful and has achieved nearly every accolade you can imagine with the Company. Kim is a refined and beautiful person who lives in a magnificent home, but when she began her Mary Kay business she was not the polished gem she is today. Kim was very much the diamond in the rough. When she was presented with the opportunity for a Mary Kay facial, Kim was a recent newlywed who had dropped out of nursing school to work two full-time jobs to help put her husband through school. She and her husband Phil lived in a twenty-year-old dilapidated trailer and she drove a Ford Pinto. Kim was worn out from her schedule and her self-esteem was at an all time low. She was not the picture of a sharp businesswoman that most people would believe could be a superstar. But the patient at the hospital at which Kim worked offered her a facial and did not judge her. She didn't think that Kim was broke so she couldn't be a woman of influence. She simply saw Kim as the kind young woman she was, and told her about the Mary Kay opportunity. Kim made the choice that if this lady believed enough in her to ask her to try this business, then she could believe in herself a little too and give it a chance. Kim soon replaced her income from her two full-time jobs and was able to quit them and devote her time to her Mary Kay business. She has since earned the use of several pink Cadillacs, earned trips all over the world, and has built a dream home on three and a half acres of land. All because one lady saw past the worn out girl who drove her worn out car home to her worn out trailer. One lady did not judge Kim, but knew that she had as much potential as anyone she would ever meet.

And what about the Beauty Consultant that I invited to the first beauty show in my home? I still have no idea why she asked my friend to be a Mary Kay Independent Beauty Consultant and not me. Maybe she thought I wasn't interested or that I didn't look like the kind of lady that would want a Mary Kay business. Whatever the reason is, she made a judgment not to ask me to consider Mary Kay as a business, that judgment certainly cost her financially and could have cost me the opportunity of a lifetime. Thank goodness the opportunity crossed my path again; because I believe that everything happens for a reason, I'm sure it was the right time for me to begin my business when I did. Yet I cannot help but think how that one judgment could have affected many lives so profoundly.

The great French poet La Fontaine said,

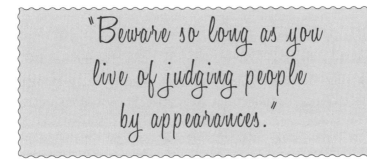

"Beware so long as you live of judging people by appearances."

One of the wonderful things I have experienced in my life through my Mary Kay business is that judging anyone is useless. I have sat at seminars in Dallas, Texas, and watched enthusiastically every year as thousands of people promenade across that Mary Kay stage and get rewarded with jewelry, trips, money, and earn the use of career cars that they have earned throughout the year. The one thing that always strikes me is how different they all are. I have seen grandmothers in wheelchairs get diamond rings. I have seen young women pick up keys to cars. I have seen every shape, size, and color being rewarded for excelling at the Mary Kay business. I have heard women speak that could hardly speak English and I have seen them cry tears of joy that someone believed in them enough to share a business opportunity with them. I have learned that there is no cookie cutter for a successful person; looking to find them for your business is futile. Success comes from within. If you judge the package you can miss the prize. I don't believe in judging anyone because I know I don't liked to be judged. I prefer to leave the judging up to God. But what I know is that if you judge the people in your business and you base your expectations on what you see, you can be disappointed. You can have successful-looking people fail you and you will have denied others the chance to prove you wrong. Mahatma Gandhi was a small, soft-spoken man who often walked barefoot and rarely raised his voice. He did not look imposing in the least, but he was a huge figure in gaining independence for India from the British. He was often judged by his appearance and underestimated nearly every time. If there is no jury, then who are we to judge?

Think Abundantly

I have heard a story and I don't know if it is true, but it makes a fantastic point. The story says that legendary golfer Arnold Palmer once played a series of exhibition matches in Saudi Arabia. The king was so impressed by his abilities that he wanted to give Mr. Palmer a present—anything Palmer asked for. Arnold Palmer initially declined saying that it was an honor to play the beautiful courses and to be treated with such awesome hospitality, but the king insisted. After he thought a while, he decided to ask for a modest gift from the oil-rich king. He asked for a golf club as a memento of his visit. The king agreed and Mr. Palmer left the country wondering what kind of club the king would give him. He thought he might get a jewel embossed driver or a solid gold putter. For several weeks he didn't get anything until one day he was called to the door to sign for a certified letter from the king of Saudi Arabia. In the envelope he found the deed to a sprawling golf country club. It appears the king of Saudi Arabia was thinking more abundantly than Arnold Palmer was at that time.

Often times we fail to think of how great we can be, and

I firmly believe that God has planted the seeds of greatness in each one of us. It is our duty to nurture those seeds, helping them to grow and become the absolute best "us" we can be. At the same time it is our privilege to seek out the seeds of greatness in others. Many people live their lives thinking that they can't be anything great. Maybe they have been told that by their family, or maybe life has been tough for them and they are happy to just be where they are. Many have simply grown weary of striving for anything more. Still others just get in a rut of providing for their family or doing the same old job that pays the bills—they forget that they used to dream of great things. I love the commercial on television that shows the children as they look to the camera and say things like, "One day I want to be in middle management," or "I want to be a 'yes' man." That commercial reminds me that we never dreamed of mediocrity. We never dreamed to settle into that rut. I have learned that there are not extraordinary people. There are only people with extraordinary drive and determination; people with visions and dreams too strong to ignore. There are people who decide that no one else will determine their future for them. People like Richard Branson, an average kid who started a mail order record business in his teens and has grown his Virgin name brand and empire into one of the largest conglomerates in the world, making himself a billionaire by taking risks. Mr. Branson's latest endeavor, Virgin Galactic, is to begin building a spaceport in New Mexico in 2008 and is pre-selling tickets to fly into space as a tourist! He was told at every turn that he would fail, that his ideas were too radical and too crazy, but his abundant thinking and determination proved the doubters wrong at every turn.

My favorite example of course is Mary Kay Ash. She knew that in most companies in 1950s, American women were not getting the same opportunities as men. She experienced the discrimination and the glass ceiling first hand. She watched as men she had trained passed her on the corporate ladder simply because of gender. But she did not just think abundantly for herself. She thought every woman in the world deserved the chance at an abundant lifestyle. So, she took her lifesavings of $5,000 and started Mary Kay Cosmetics with the goal of enriching women's lives. The company she started now has more than a million Independent Beauty Consultants in more than thirty markets all over the world, and has touched the lives of countless millions throughout the last forty years. I am sure if she was alive today, Mary Kay would be excited about the success and the growth of the Company, but she would not be surprised or intimidated by it. She was the most abundant thinker I have ever met and she instilled the abundance mentality in me. While she was a very conservative woman personally, and was constantly telling us to save our money and to be smart and frugal businesswomen, she also made sure we knew that the sky was the limit when it came to how far we could take the opportunity she provided for us.

Just think: if there are great things happening to anyone anywhere in the world, it can be happening to you. You have to open your mind up to be ready to receive abundance. You have to be ready to say, "Yes, I deserve that as much as anyone." Once you prepare yourself for abundance and open your heart and mind to accept it, then you can freely think abundantly and expect greatness to come to you. When you think abundantly you combine it with the positive thinking we discussed earlier to tell yourself about all the abundance that comes to you. Instead of ever saying, "I just never have enough money," you pop your rubber band on your wrist because that was a negative affirmation. Then you replace that thought with an abundant positive affirmation like, "I always have more than enough money because I am smart and charitable with it. In fact, money is always flowing to me in abundant quantities because I am a good steward of money and I deserve abundance." It may sound hokey, but living abundantly isn't an accident. Living abundantly is a result of consistently doing the right things with a positive attitude. Living abundantly isn't about an inexhaustible amount of money either. It is about always having more than enough. More than enough of everything. I am rarely late because I know I always have more than enough time. I have more than enough time to get to the airport even though traffic seems worse than normal. I have more than enough energy to take pictures with everyone that needs one. I have more than enough empathy to listen to a friend when pain has entered her life. I have more than enough courage to face the things I must face in order to eliminate fear from my life. I have more than enough faith to turn over to God the things of this world that I cannot understand. I have learned to think abundantly and abundance has filled my life in every positive way imaginable and I am thankful for it. One of my great friends, who is like a daughter to me, is an offspring Independent National Sales Director, Donna

Meixsell. She is a master of abundant thinking. Her philosophy is simple. She has nicknamed herself "All-Out Donna Meixsell". She calls herself that because whatever she does, she does with an abundance mentality. She is one hundred percent committed to whatever activity she is doing. She gives of herself abundantly in order to receive abundance in her life. If she is talking to me on the phone, she is one hundred percent engaged with our conversation. If she is spending time with her daughter Madison and her husband Berrae, she is one hundred percent involved with them. If she is working she is one hundred percent focused on what is going on in her business; if she is relaxing, she is one hundred percent relaxing without distraction. Donna expects abundance in her life and she gives abundance in everything she does. This enables her to receive it in return. Her dedication to her family, her church, her friends, and her business is unquestionable and she is rewarded for it by always having more than enough.

Step Out of Your Comfort Zone

Do you remember ever having pains in your legs as a child and going to your parents to complain, just to have them tell you they were growing pains? All of a sudden you felt better because you realized that if what they were saying was true, all you had to do was tough it out and you'd be closer to being all grown up. Guess what? There is no such thing as all grown up. Even though we may have gotten as tall as we will ever be, as long as we live, we have the capacity to grow. And sometimes it still hurts. In 1978 the United States Air Force transferred us to Las Vegas, Nevada, and I was a little nervous about how the move would affect my business, because there was only one Sales Director, Arlene Dennis, in the entire area. Talk about stepping out of my comfort zone. I knew I would have to really focus if I wanted to continue to grow my business. I learned so much from that experience. I learned that I could trust my abilities and that women everywhere wanted to be a part of this fabulous Company. During the course of my Mary Kay business our area developed more than thirty Sales Directors in Las Vegas, and there are currently about 100 Mary Kay Independent Sales Directors in the Las Vegas area. I had to step way out of my comfort zone, but the reward was well worth it.

If your goal doesn't make you feel sick to your stomach when you have to stand up and tell it to a crowd, then it isn't big enough. I remind my business partners of this all the time. The comforting thing is that Edward Teller tells us, "When you come to the end of all the light you know, and it's time to step into the darkness of the unknown, faith is knowing that one of two things shall happen: Either you will be given something solid to stand on or you will be taught to fly." Because of that, most dreams become realities. So many people want a life of their own that is not dictated by their company, or the state they work for, or the spouse they live with. People want to take a chance, but they are so scared of what lies on the other side of that door that they never bother.

Mary Kay said, "Most people live and die with their music still unplayed. They never dare to try." I want every person who ever hears me, every person who ever reads this book, or every person who ever hears of Mary Kay to know that, whether or not they have a Mary Kay business they have a dream worth fulfilling—a dream outside of getting up and going to work everyday. There are people who have died who are better painters than Picasso, better musicians than Mozart, better writers than Hemmingway, and better actors than Brando, but they never let their talent shine. What a travesty to see wasted talent; what a worse travesty to never see that talent at all. As I have said before, I believe that God has planted the seeds of greatness in all of us and it is our duty to cultivate that seed. I hope for every person to step out of their comfort zone and become something more. I was so terrified the first time I had to speak to a group of twenty people. I was nervous and I felt like I was going to forget everything I planned to say. The same thing happened when I needed to speak to a group of a hundred people, then five hundred people, then one thousand. Then I had to speak in front of a Seminar crowd of five thousand people. Every single time I was stepping out of my comfort zone. I was stepping into the unknown abyss and I knew one of two things would happen to me: I would either be given something solid to stand on, or I would be given wings so that I could fly. Every time I made it. I haven't died from giving a speech yet, regardless of what I may have told you if you asked me when I first started. If you look at all of the amazing accomplishments, you will find a person who was undoubtedly scared, but had the courage to step one foot out of their comfort zone.

We recently lost a great civil rights pioneer, Rosa Parks. She walked onto a bus, sat down, and at the next stop was asked to move to the back by a white person (as a black woman in the United States at that time, she was expected to comply). But she decided she would not relinquish her seat. Do you imagine that she was so comfortable on a hard city bus seat that she felt too relaxed to give it up? I am certain that that was probably the most uncomfortable seat she had in her entire life! She sat in that seat when her comfort zone was in the back of the bus with the other African American passengers, but she decided that she would step out of her comfort zone and stay in her seat, regardless of the consequences. Thinking of her sitting in that seat with the jeers and ridicule she was forced to endure to make a statement about racial equality in the United States makes me laugh to think that I was ever afraid to walk up to another lady and ask her if she had ever tried Mary Kay products.

Think of the pioneers of our world. Think of Christopher Columbus sailing off into the horizon when most people thought he would fall off the edge of the earth. Think of Copernicus who was ridiculed because he thought the earth revolved around the sun. Think of Martin Luther King, Jr., who believed that all men are created equal. He was beaten, arrested, jailed, and eventually assassinated for daring to step out of his comfort zone. Why is it that so many of us are scared to take a chance on ourselves when the consequences are minimal, especially when there are those who risked everything for what they believed to be true? I think it is because they knew there was something better beyond that comfort zone. There was a mission to accomplish and a dream to fulfill. Throughout history slaves have fought to be freed, women have fought to vote, and men have fought to go to the moon—but these were not the dreams of a group. They were the dreams of a few people who dared to step outside their comfort zones to make big things happen. They stepped out regardless of their risks of failure. They stepped out because of basic belief in themselves. They had confidence and faith that they could accomplish what they set out to do. I have that faith in every person I ever speak to. You could be the next youngest, or greatest, Mary Kay Independent National Sales Director. You can become the next anything you want to be.

The first step is the hardest. If you stand on the top of a huge hill and look down at the steep, grassy face of that hill, you might think to yourself, I am going to fall all the way down this hill and break my neck. If so, you will never get down that hill—no matter what is at the bottom. If you were standing on the top of that same hill and somebody told you that at the bottom was financial security for you and your family for the rest of your lives, and you could look down there and see it, would you think you could never make it? Or would you take that first step off of the hill and slide, tumble, fall forward, or whatever you had to do to bring financial security to you and your family? I know what I would do. I would make a plan, and equip myself with all of the tools it would take me to get down that hill. Then I would use that plan to step off the ledge—out of my comfort zone—and charge my way towards that prize. I know because I have been there. I have stepped out of my comfort zone. Do you think a home economics teacher from Bogue Chitto, Mississippi, was always prepared to be a top Mary Kay Independent National Sales Director? At one time I was nervous about being a captain's wife and attending military functions. But I stepped out of my comfort zone. I became a top Sales Director and a top National Sales Director because I stepped out on faith and conviction that I wanted more and needed more in my life. I believed I was as good as God had made anyone else. So are you.

Find a Mentor

I have certainly been blessed with wonderful mentors in my life; however, I don't believe they became my mentors by accident. My first and greatest mentor was Mary Kay Ash. When I first saw her on stage in Chicago in January of 1976, I felt as if I met her face to face by just being in the same room with her. She was fun, intelligent, and full of vitality; she seemed to be bigger than life. That day I set a goal to get Mary Kay Ash to know my name. From then on whenever I won prizes or attended functions at which I would see Mary Kay, I said to her, "Hi, Mary Kay. I'm Pat Fortenberry." After I earned the use of my second pink Cadillac, I walked up to her on stage and she looked at me, smiled, and said, "I *know* who you are, Pat Fortenberry." I was so proud. As I continued in my business and moved up the ladder of success, I was fortunate enough to get to spend quite a bit of time with Mary Kay. She really became a personal mentor for me. Even if I had never been able to spend that time with her, I would have emulated her integrity, her love for people, her dedication to the company, and her priorities of faith first, family second, and career third. I knew that she was the kind of person who I wanted to be, and I took every speech I heard her give as if it were written with me in mind. I cherished the wisdom she shared.

I also found mentors who I could emulate in my daily business, like my adopted Sales Director Miriam Alexander, who encouraged me and believed in me until I could believe in myself. Once I became a National Sales Director, I had to find mentors who could guide me along that path as well. Thankfully, I found my sister National Sales Directors, Emily Mclaughlin, Carolyn Ward, Sally Rattray, Joanne Holman, Cheryl Warfield, and Virginia Robirds, who have not only served to guide me along my path and help me excel further than I ever could have alone, but have also become terrific friends, confidants, and travel partners along the way. I have also found mentors outside of Mary Kay who have helped me develop as a leader and a person. John Maxwell is one of those mentors, whose books on leadership and success have inspired me to seek him out as a speaker and teacher for my events and as a personal mentor for me.

As strong as we all want to be, there are times when even the most stalwart of us needs a confidant to lean on. In times of doubt we need a hand to reach up to, a hand that will reassure us that we are going to make it and deserve the success that we are striving for. That is why we have mentors. Sometimes our friends can fill those roles, but in our business it is best to have a mentor who knows specifically why our struggles are worthwhile. A mentor will encourage us to push through the challenges when a friend, with all good intentions, may want us to step back or take an easier path that can take us away from our goals. A mentor can help you avoid the distractions or mistakes and can help you navigate your business in a caring but more objective way than a friend can. Mentors can repaint the big picture for you and seemingly reach in their front pocket and pull out the dream of success you may have misplaced and give it back to you. Friends empathize while mentors inspire!

Be a Mentor

As an Independent Executive Senior Sales Director, I once went to a Career Conference at the Disneyland Hotel in California. I was plotting my way to becoming an Independent National Sales Director. One of the first National Sales Directors in the Company, Helen McVoy, sat down with me for more than an hour and helped me chart my course. What I have always remembered about that conversation is not so much what she said, but the fact that she took the time and the interest in me when it was of no benefit to her at all in her business. Then I realized that the benefit to her was that she was fulfilling what her heart wanted her to do—pass on her wisdom to others and mentor someone who needed it. I have followed the examples set for me by the wonderful mentors I have had in my life to the best of my ability. I have been a mentor to those who need me and those who will accept my advice. It is my sincerest opinion that we all have some very special gifts to give to others who need exactly what we are offering. I also know that being a mentor and giving of yourself can be one of the most fulfilling things you will ever do. Mary Kay said, "We must have a theme, a goal, a purpose in our lives. If you don't know where you're aiming, you don't have a goal. My goal is to live my life in such a way that when I die, someone can say, she cared."

One of my greatest joys is watching a woman become a wonderful mentor herself. Witnessing this evolution gave me such pride and security; knowing that my business would continue to grow because those people whom I was educating were passing on to others the valuable lessons I had learned from those who had mentored me. I know all of the Sales Directors and National Sales Directors in my area have become wonderful mentors in their own right; and it has made me so proud. Independent Executive Senior Sales Directors Jeanenne Lumpkin and Jeannette Cochran as well as Independent Future Executive Senior Sales Director Jan McCluer have been shining examples of women who have been in my Area since I debuted as an Independent National Sales Director in 1984. I have been able to watch these women grow, learn and develop into wonderful leaders who have mentored untold numbers of women through their businesses and lives. I am so proud to have worked with them for so many years and even more proud to call them my friends.

Being a mentor can also be a wonderful learning experience. When you know that someone is depending on you for guidance and direction, it forces you to thoroughly examine the things you have done and find the lessons in your successes and your challenges. When you can point out to someone else a better way to handle a situation, you can know how to better handle similar situations in the future. Being a teacher means that first you must learn; that is a journey that never ends.

Make Me Feel Important

Mary Kay told us on countless occasions to treat every person as if they have a sign around their neck that says, "Make me feel important." I have always thought what a wonderful world we would live in if more people followed this simple advice. We all know that feeling needed and important is a basic emotional need of every human being on the planet. Feeling important helps us to keep going when it would be easier to stop. It helps us to give of ourselves because we have already been deemed important by someone else. Think of how good you feel when coworkers or family members acknowledge how special you are to them and how invaluable you are to their success. Now think of how many times a day you can spread that feeling to others. So many people go through their day, their year, their life rarely hearing how important they are. If you are the person that gives them that satisfaction and that bit of encouragement, just think what a difference you make in their life! I make it a goal of mine to give gifts and recognition to everyone in my life as often as possible.

My grandchildren think it is completely normal to get presents for St. Patrick's Day, Thanksgiving, and the Fourth of July as well as the traditional gift-giving holidays like Christmas and birthdays. I don't give them presents to spoil them; I give them presents because I want them to know that I love them and am always thinking about them. I want them to know that they are important to me; I want them to feel special. But anyone who has ever known me knows that this philosophy extends to everyone with whom I work. When we have an event, I have prizes and recognition for just about everyone involved. You should see the surprised looks I get when I have the people attending my events applaud the staff of the hotel for their excellent service. I want them to feel special for the work they do. I would imagine at convention centers the staff goes to work day in and day out and the conventioneers rarely even acknowledge the fact that there are actual people preparing and bringing them their food and drinks. Well, I want those people to know that we do notice their hard work and our events could not be as successful without their hard work—so it becomes our goal to make them feel special. I always have gifts for those who help me organize and set up my events because I want them to feel special.

It has been my experience that just about everyone loves recognition. Even the people who seem really shy and withdrawn, even though they may be a little embarrassed at the time, love the fact that their accomplishments did not go unnoticed. Donna Meixsell tells a story of how, when she first started her Mary Kay business, she would go to weekly success meetings. She saw ladies getting ribbons for their accomplishments and how excited they would be about those "silly little ribbons" as she would call them. But what she will admit is that they were only "silly little ribbons" because she wasn't getting any. Once Donna began really working her business and began getting the ribbons herself, it was amazing how those "silly little ribbons" became badges of honor and—to her surprise!—she was just as excited about them as anyone. They made Donna feel special. Now Donna never fails to recognize the accomplishments of others no matter how small they may be because she has seen how different it can make someone feel.

Mary Kay once told me of how, before she began her Company, she won the opportunity to go to a dinner for the top sales people in her company. At this dinner, she got a chance to meet the president of the company. Mary Kay stood in line for hours waiting for her turn to meet the president of the company. When at long last she got to the front of the receiving line, the president held out his hand to shake Mary Kay's; as he did, he looked right past her at how long the line was and she was shuffled right on past him. He made her feel completely insignificant. From then on, she knew that if she were ever in charge she would never look past a single person. She always made a point when meeting with someone to look them right in the eye and make them feel like the only person in the room. Mary Kay also made people feel special by always taking the time to take pictures with those who wanted them. She would stand for hours just about everywhere she went in order to allow people the opportunity to have their picture taken with the founder of the Company. I know I cherish the pictures I have with Mary Kay. She always made me feel special and I attempt to do the same for all of those who never got to meet Mary Kay.

Find Your "Why"

Self-motivation may be the single most elusive trait in the human spirit. Of course there are those rare people who seem single-minded of purpose and can do whatever they set their mind to regardless of the task. Glenn McCarroll, Independent National Sales Director Kelly McCarroll's husband, is a world-class athlete. He has competed in the Ironman Triathlons all over the world. The Ironman series challenges athletes to swim 2.4 miles, bike 112 miles, and then run a marathon of 26.2 miles—all in one day! To complete any one of these components is more than most of us will accomplish in our lives, but Glenn not only finishes the course, but he is racing against other athletes the whole time. To endure such a rigorous event Glenn has to train everyday. He may get up at 4:30 in the morning and swim a mile in the open ocean, then bike forty or fifty miles, then round off his day with a ten-mile run. He doesn't train like this once in a while, he trains practically every day. Certainly there are days that the bed feels extra comfortable and sleeping in till 10:00 a.m. would be great but you will rarely find Glenn taking a day off.

You might wonder how there are people out there like that, then there are the rest of us. Well, I can assure you Glenn is not from another planet. Even better, I can tell you that I believe there is nothing significantly different between the Ironman triathlete that trains every morning at 4:30, and anyone that may pick up this book and flip through these pages. The only difference is the highly trained athlete has found his "why." Your "why" is that thing, person, or reason that will make you do what you don't feel like doing when you don't feel like doing it. When you find your "why" for whatever it is that you want to accomplish, then there is nothing that can keep you from doing it. For many of us our "why" is our family. I have seen women overcome amazing obstacles and do things they never thought they could do to provide a better life for their family or a college education for their children. If you told me when I started my Mary Kay business that someday I would have to stand and speak to a crowd of 5,000 people at a Seminar or even to fifty people at an event, I would have run the other way. But what I loved more than anything were Pam, Craig, and Charles. I wanted to make some extra money so when Easter came around I would not have to dip into our food budget to get an Easter dress for Pam and a suit for Craig. Charles was already working hard as an officer in the Air Force and I knew I would do anything if it meant being able to provide just that little extra money for my family. Throughout the time I worked my Mary Kay business I never wanted to miss a single baseball game, golf match, or anything my family was doing—and I rarely did. When I missed anything I knew they were the reason I was going the extra mile and holding the extra skin care class. I have been able to give my family a wonderful life and help them experience some of the most beautiful places in the world; there is nothing I would not do for them because they are my "why." Along the way I have realized that I have gotten a great deal of fulfillment out of my accomplishments. I drive myself to be the best I can be. But I would have never been able to get to that point without fighting through the times when it would have been easier—to stay in bed or not venture out into the snowy St. Louis night—without my three "whys" to think about.

Rhonda Fraczkowski is a beautiful and very faithful Independent National Sales Director in my Mary Kay family. When I say faithful I mean that she is full of spiritual faith, the best kind of faithful. When I first met Rhonda she was a new Independent Beauty Consultant in Mary Kay. She came to Seminar in Dallas one year a bit unsure whether or not she wanted to move up the career path with her Mary Kay business. Something caught her attention at that Seminar and she returned home with a new vision. She saw that her Mary Kay business could pay the way for her two beautiful children, Ben and Morgan, to go to a private, Christian school without putting the entire financial burden on her husband, Eddie, who was building his own company at the time. She had found her "why" and from then on, focus and determination was no problem for Rhonda. The next year Rhonda earned the use of the signature Mary Kay Pink Cadillac, promoted herself to the position of an Independent Sales Director, and returned to Seminar as the Queen of Sharing for our Seminar. Once you find your "why," "how" isn't nearly the problem it seems to be.

For some people, their "why" is internal. It is a desire to be the best at something, to be number one, or even to be part of something bigger than they themselves are. Other people find their "why" in the doubts of others. I have seen mildly interested consultants catch fire and plow full steam ahead because a spouse voiced doubt that they could succeed. Some people envision a lifestyle that they can only obtain through hard work. That vision sustains them to work long hours and to get out of bed when the body is saying "stay, sleep."

I understand it's easy enough for me to simply tell you to find your "why," but what may be harder is for you to know how. If you already know what your "why" is then that is fantastic. Learn to focus on it and use it constantly to motivate you to do the things you don't want to do and soon, before doubt or procrastination can slip into your mind, your "why" will jump to the forefront and get you moving. If you don't know what your "why" is I can show you how you can find it.

Take a sheet of paper and draw a big circle on it. This will become the wheel of your perfect life. The spokes of the wheel will be the most important aspects of your life: health, finances, family, professional, personal, spiritual, and any others that you feel don't fall into any other category. Underneath each of these spokes list everything you want to be, have, or do in your life. Whatever you do, do not limit yourself here. Dream as big as you want to dream. Remember, people told Bill Gates that even if he could make a computer small enough to fit on someone's desktop, the general public wouldn't want one and would never learn how to use one! As the richest man in the world with a personal fortune of more than $50 billion, I guess we all know how Bill Gates' dream is turning out. You can list small accomplishments all the way to the most audacious thing you could ever think of. Once you have your lists, I want you to really focus on each one and take your time to really find out what dreams are the most important to you in each category. Pick the ones that you honestly believe would make you a happier, more complete person when you accomplished them. From these most important things, you can build your affirmations. As I mentioned earlier, what you think about you talk about, what you talk about you bring about. Your affirmations are a list of statements that discuss your dreams as if they are already happening. You write out your affirmations on a piece of paper, picture-frame style. This means instead of writing one line under the other, you write to the edge of the paper then turn the paper sideways and continue. As you write, your affirmations will spiral in tighter and tighter. Writing your affirmations in this pattern helps you focus when you go back to read them. If they are written out the regular way, you may find your mind wandering or just going through the motions as you read them. When you write your affirmations, you need to make them very specific, even with the date.

For example, a new Mary Kay Independent Beauty Consultant may write an affirmation that says, "I am a Mary Kay Independent National Sales Director by Seminar 2009 because I do my business the right way and constantly attract motivated people to me who want more and need more in their lives." Or a mother may write, "Our family is always a happy, close knit family because we always make time for each other and we uplift each other everyday." Someone overweight may have and affirmation of, "I am a perfect size six because everyday I only eat small portions of healthy food." It may be far fetched, but that is the idea. When you read your affirmations and focus on them every day, you bring them closer to reality because you will think about them more, talk about them more, and accomplish them more. You will notice in the affirmation examples I have listed there are only positive words. The words "don't," "not," or "never" are withheld from our affirmations because we don't want any negativity in our affirmations. You don't want your subconscious to hear the rest of the sentence. For example, if you say, "I am never late," your subconscious can still make a mistake and hear "I am late." If everything is positive then your mind can only hear what you tell it, like, "I always arrive on time for all of my appointments." These affirmations contain your "whys." When you read them everyday you will begin to self-motivate to accomplish all of the things in your life you want to accomplish. As your affirmations become reality, make them bigger and better—you will find yourself watching less television and actively pursuing your dreams more.

Set Your Goals

A goal is only a wish without a time limit.

Following a chapter about finding your "why" and writing your affirmations is the perfect place to discuss my favorite topic—setting goals. Let me correct that, this chapter we will discuss achieving goals. You see, I do not believe much of anything gets accomplished without a goal, a plan, and a time limit. On May 25, 1961, President Kennedy addressed congress and said, "I believe that this nation should commit itself to achieving the goal, before this decade is out, of landing a man on the moon and returning him safely to the earth." On July 20, 1969, Neil Armstrong accomplished the feat and completed the goal. What a fantastic example of setting a tremendous goal with a definite time limit then making it happen. With the rest of his speech that day, President Kennedy laid out a specific plan for how the space program would be funded and what intermediate goals would be expected. In one memorable speech, President Kennedy set a goal that inspired millions: a time limit in which to accomplish the goal and a plan to tie it all together and make it happen. His ability to lead and inspire is one of the reasons he remains so revered to this day.

I believe there are three kinds of goals. There are short-range goals, medium-range goals, and long-term goals. But no matter the range of goals, they first have to be written down. A significantly greater percentage of goals that are written down are accomplished as opposed to the goals never written down. That is why I strongly recommend to all of my people that they always keep their goals in front of them. I start my year by deciding what my short-range, medium-range, and long-range goals are for the year. I print them off and plaster them all over my house. Some people think I just tell other people to post their goals because I have supposedly "made it." But if you were to walk into my home this very instant, you would see my goals in every bathroom, over the kitchen sink, and in my bedroom. Anywhere I go I see my goals. I keep them with me at all times so I never forget what I am working towards. I spend so much time at other Mary Kay peoples' home that I expect to see their goals all over the house; when people who aren't affiliated with Mary Kay come to my home and they see these tiny posters up and ask me what they are, it almost takes me aback. "They're goal posters of course," I tell them.

I knew I was doing a good job as a mother and a GiGi (I don't consider myself a grandmother) when my daughter told the story of my granddaughter Katie's goal poster experience. It was a rainy day and Katie and her friends couldn't play outside. They came to Pam wondering what they could do. Pam, knowing that little girls love arts and crafts, gave them some poster board, magazines, markers, and tape, then told them to make goal posters for themselves. A few hours later the children came down and wanted to show off their goal posters. The first two girls were as you would expect—pony rides for their birthday, new clothes, and a few of the most popular toys. But Katie's goal poster had a big picture of a swimming pool and underneath she had written "this year." Then she had a picture of a huge house on the water and underneath it said, "in five years." Then she had a picture of a girl driving a Lamborghini and underneath it said, "in my thirties." She made that without coaching from her mother or me, but she had been around us so much that she understood that she needed to have short-range goals, medium-range goals, and long-range goals. She also knew that those goals had to be bigger than she could imagine. As the grandmother of this ten year old, I am so excited that she is setting her sights so high.

Consistency Is the Key to Success

Have you ever thought of the dedication it takes to be an Olympic athlete? Could you imagine every single day waking up and training for one event? The way you eat is tailored to your workout. The way you sleep is monitored by a coach. Every movement you make while training is scrutinized to find a way to give you a little more speed, a fraction of an inch more distance, or cut your wind resistance the tiniest bit. Now imagine that this is your life for four whole years and that around the world thousands of others just like you are working to be just a little bit better. Then there is the realization that after all that training and mental preparation, it will all be over in a few minutes; only one person out of those thousands who have put in years of training, only one, will stand atop a podium and have a gold medal placed around his or her neck. Then once that is over, that person starts training for the next Olympics in four more years.

With that kind of desire to succeed, do you think they take the first three weeks off every month and then work really hard for that last week? I have met Consultants and Sales Directors that run their businesses this way. Part of the reason for this is the fact that with Mary Kay, or any direct sales organization, the best part and the worst part is that you are in business for yourself—you are your own boss. As the boss, if you choose to procrastinate or be distracted there is no one to tell you to get back to business. Success is formed daily, not in a day. And just like the elite athlete, you can find success in your daily routine. Frank Sinatra used to call himself an overnight success that took thirty years to happen. The truth is that no one is an overnight success. Anyone who becomes a success has worked tirelessly at perfecting whatever it is they do, most of the time for little or no recognition until the right people see or hear their work and reward them overnight for it. I know that achieving my goals was like eating an elephant. Do you know how you can eat an elephant? One bite at a time. I set goals that seemed like they would be impossible when I set them but I knew if I got up each day and did all the things I needed to do in that day to get me closer to my goal, then I could reach those goals.

When I first began my Mary Kay business, Charles and I were going over all of the materials and the career path. We decided that if I held ten classes a month every month then I could go anywhere I wanted with my Mary Kay business. So at the beginning of every month I would put a calendar on the refrigerator and would mark off my skin care classes as I held them. When I got to ten, we would take the children out for ice cream. I think my son, Craig, learned to count to ten by marking off my skin care classes so he could get more ice cream. Of course the ten classes weren't all I was doing with my business. I never missed weekly meeting. We always called them "success meetings" because the people that always came were the ones who wanted to become successful. I never missed one that I can remember. Mary Kay used to tell us that if you miss one meeting you're sick, if you miss two meetings in row you're dying, and if you miss three in a row you're dead. Aside from the occasional metaphorical resurrection, she was right. My dear friend, Independent Senior National Sales Director Linda McBroom, used to come to the meetings with me every week in the beginning. She had come in with a small order and really wasn't working her business at all, but every week she would be there. Now she is an Inner Circle Senior National Sales Director and is among the top Independent National Sales Directors in the Company. When I tell this story people always ask Linda why she kept coming to the meetings when she wasn't really working her business and she tells them, "Pat was my friend and I knew she would be there, and I didn't want to disappoint her." Linda, of course, has never disappointed me—I think something must have caught fire in her at one of those meetings to spur her to her success of today. But I hate to think what would have happened if she had not been consistent about coming to those meetings. It reminds me of a quote from Jim Ryun, who in 1966 was the first high school runner to break the four-minute mile barrier. He said, "Motivation is what gets you started. Habit is what keeps you going."

Whenever I talk about consistency, I always talk about Independent National Sales Director Kimberly Copeland. I introduced Kimberly to our Fortenberry Area "Inner Circle program," which is a program Mary Kay always taught us to help us stay consistent. The inner circle is where you have people commit to a weekly quota of appointments, interviews, and retail product sales. This program helps people obtain balance in their business and consistency. There were three programs 2+2+2, 3+3+3, and 5+5+5. Kimberly Copeland loves this program If they say, "How can I be successful?" Kimberly tells them what formula she used "Five skin care appointments, five interviews, and $500 in sales each week." Kimberly worked this program consistently for herself, became a Sales Director, and earned the use of her first pink Cadillac. Her second year she helped ten other women become Mary Kay Independent Sales Directors and earned her place in the Circle of Excellence on the Seminar stage. In 2003, her third **year,** she became the youngest National Sales Director in the history of the company. Kimberly is a model of consistency. She set her goals and used the Fortenberry Area Inner Circle as a plan to reach those goals. She knows that a goal without action is just a wish.

Speed Bumps Are Not Stop Signs

It has been said that a winner is the failure who tried one more time, and the failure is the winner who didn't. It is estimated that Thomas Edison failed at inventing the incandescent light bulb more than 10,000 times before he finally succeeded. Now what do we consider Mr. Edison? A failure? Absolutely not! We consider him a tremendous success and the founder of General Electric, the world's largest company. But even he stumbled a few times before claiming his success. As a matter of fact he is quoted as saying about his work on the light bulb, "I have not failed, I have only found 10,000 ways that won't work." Can you imagine where we would be if he had given up after 9,999 tries? Certainly, no one would fault a person for quitting after so many attempts. Thomas Edison was not afraid of his failures. He examined each one of them very carefully and learned from each and every mistake he made; then he went back to the drawing board and tried to devise a way to overcome the challenge in front of him. He knew the difference between a stumbling block and a stop sign. He realized that quitting was the only true way to fail. He told us this when he said, "Many of life's failures are people who did not realize how close they were to success when they gave up."

There have been times in my business when I felt like maybe I was spinning my wheels and not getting to where I wanted to be. Maybe the "no's" were piling up and my confidence was wearing thin, but I realized that what I was doing was nothing like inventing the light bulb. I was selling makeup and sharing a wonderful opportunity; as long as the women I was talking to had skin then I could be a success. If I had listened to that little voice in my head that said, *This just isn't working out; we have failed at this makeup thing. Maybe we should see what else is out there,* then where would I be? I would certainly not be a Mary Kay millionaire. I would have probably gone back to teaching home economics and continued to think of myself as a failure at sales. But I knew that just down the road from the stumbling blocks of failure is the onramp to the success expressway. And as long as I didn't imagine a stop sign, I could make it … and I did.

Perseverance isn't the only key to not quitting. I have talked to so many people who were facing hardships; in a defeated voice through clinched teeth, they have looked at me and said, "But I haven't quit." The only problem with that statement is it isn't complete. It should be, "I haven't quit … going through the motions." Winston Churchill said, "Success is going from failure to failure without losing enthusiasm." When I encounter someone who tells me all the things that have gone wrong and then gives me the half-hearted, "But I haven't quit," I know that is someone who needs a little more attention, a little more unconditional love, and probably a little coaching. You see, going through the motions isn't really doing anything. Without enthusiasm and passion for what you are doing, you can only improve your situation by luck. If you happen to stumble across that one person who needs exactly what you are offering and was going to get it from the next person they bumped into that had it anyway, then you are in luck. That can turn your attitude around in an instant. But a far more effective way to do any kind of business is to never just go through the motions. People can sense the energy you are giving out. Whether it is in person, in front of a group, on the phone, or even on television, people can sense what is going on in your head most of the time. When you are just going through the motions, the energy you send out is negative, desperate, and unattractive. You may not have let your stumbling blocks lead you to a stop sign but they probably have you in the lane for an exit ramp. When you are just going through the motions you can create more stumbling blocks for yourself, and it can be a vicious cycle. I know in sales we always like to talk about the numbers. Companies go to great lengths to tell new sales people the "closing averages" for their product. Let's imagine a company tells you that on average, one in three people you talk to will buy your product. Now let's say you talk to thirty people and you just go through the motions, and on top of that you have an attitude that says, "I am having a rough time right now, nobody is buying what I am selling." Do you believe you will sell ten of whatever it is you have to sell? I would guess that you would not do it. If that were the case then no one would need sales coaching at all. Actually, companies would not need sales people at all. They would program robots to stand on the street corner and repeat their sales pitch over and over to make sales; after all what does a robot do? It just goes through the motions.

Whenever I talk to someone in my business who is just going through the motions, the first thing I do is encourage them to stop everything. Stop calling customers, stop talking to prospective recruits, stop coaching other sales people. I ask them to just stop. I believe negativity is like a virus, and I don't want them infecting everyone they come in contact with. Also, I don't believe it is fair to someone who may be genuinely interested in an opportunity to be approached by someone who is not enjoying themselves. Who wants to work with someone who isn't happy where they are? Once they have stopped, I ask them to focus on what they enjoy about their business. I ask them why they began their business in the first place, and what has changed since they were excited about their business. Most the time I realize that one of two things is happening—either they are forcing themselves to reach a goal, which leads to a sense of desperation, which comes across very negatively to customers and coworkers; or they are having problems totally unrelated to their business that is affecting how they are working. Many times just having the person talk to me, explain exactly what is going on, and allowing them to get it all off their chest can be all that person needs to refresh their outlook and recharge their batteries.

Other times people need a break to relax. It is much better to slow down and complete the race than to sprint to exhaustion and never reach the finish line. I would much rather have someone pull over at a rest area and then get back on the road than to stop altogether.

Actors have a goal to make every performance seem like the first time they have ever performed. They must have the enthusiasm for what they are doing just like they did when they first auditioned; if they don't, the audience will be able to tell and not be entertained. Just like those actors, we must have enthusiasm for what we are doing to be able to do it well. If we let our stumbling blocks discourage us, we may continue to stumble until we fall at the base of a stop sign. But if we take our stumbling blocks in stride and stay excited about what we are doing, like Thomas Edison, then it doesn't matter how many times we fall down—we will always be able to get up again, learn from our mistakes, and continue on our journey.

Whenever I think about enthusiasm and persistence, my thoughts turn to my good friend and offspring Independent National Sales Director, Kelly McCarroll. Kelly knows all about speed bumps. She has encountered challenges in her life that would leave lesser people emotionally paralyzed, but not Kelly. One day she had a beautiful family, a husband with a high-paying job, a nice home, and financial security. Virtually overnight, Kelly found herself raising two young boys on her own with no idea of how she was going to provide for them. After a very rough time working long hours and still not being able to save her house, Kelly found herself a

Mary Kay Independent Beauty Consultant. She worked with inspiration, dedication, and determination, and became a top Independent Sales Director. She was doing very well, but she wanted more. She consistently helped other women reach the position of Independent Sales Director, but obstacles in their lives caused them, one by one, to leave the Mary Kay opportunity. On her way to Seminar one year, she got a call from her last remaining Independent Sales Director who told Kelly that she was no longer going to be a Sales Director. Kelly went to Seminar with zero Sales Directors on her team, but she remained undaunted. She knew the situations she was facing were nothing compared to the speed bumps she had encountered earlier in her life. If they hadn't stopped her then, there was no way she would be stopped now. At Seminar as I spoke to my Sales Directors, I was asking them what their goals were. Without hesitation, Kelly stood up and told me that she would be my next Independent National Sales Director. To anyone reading this who is not familiar with the Mary Kay Career Path, at that time to reach the position that Kelly had claimed meant that she would have to help at least eighteen women become Independent Sales Directors. This was certainly a bold statement for her to make.

But Kelly had passion; when she spoke, people felt her enthusiasm. Anyone that listened to her knew that she would not stop until she reached her goal. Kelly left her speed bumps in the rearview mirror, never imagined a stop sign, and drove full speed ahead. Within twenty-two months Kelly did what takes most Independent National Sales Directors much longer to accomplish. Kelly McCarroll was my next Independent National Sales Director. Kelly often tells her story, and every time I hear it I am amazed. She reaches into her heart to share her experiences; each time I feel like I am hearing it for the first time. Kelly knows what it is like to overcome setbacks, and she's serious about helping others learn from her mistakes.

Be Sold Yourself

Thousands of times and hundreds of ways I have heard it said: find something you love to do and you'll never work another day in your life. Well, more than I have heard it, I have lived it. I truly love what I do. I can't tell you that I love sales and that's why I love what I do. I can't say I love the thousands of rejections I have gotten in my life that came along my path. But I do love the Company. I believe in Mary Kay Inc. . It was easy for me to buy into the Company's mission statement of "enriching women's lives." And I know in my heart that if this was not the opportunity presented to me all those years ago, I would not be as successful as I am today.

I don't care if you work for General Motors, Pfizer, Wal-mart, or even Mary Kay Inc.—if you don't believe in your product or your company you need to find another line of work. I would never want to buy a Mercedes from a sales-person who I saw driving a BMW. I know there are a lot of good salespeople in the world. I also know there are a lot of salespeople that make a lot of money selling products they don't really believe in. But at the end of the day do you think those people feel good about what they do? I also know that the percentage of salespeople who can sell products they don't believe in is very small. Those same people could probably win an Oscar if they were in the movies because they have to be fantastic actors. If you are not sold on your product or your company, how can you expect others to be sold on it? I know if it were me, whoever I talked to would know in two seconds if I didn't like Mary Kay Inc. If I don't like something, I can't get excited about it. If I can't get excited about it then how am I supposed to get anyone else excited about it? Even if I did, I wouldn't be able to sleep well at night knowing that I talked someone else into something that I knew was not a good product. Then I would have a hard time dragging myself out of bed every morning to go do it all over again. I am glad I have found something I love to do so I will never work another day in my life.

I know some of you reading this think that I am not acknowledging the challenges and the effort I have put in to what I have done. I am certainly not saying that I just woke up everyday and the commissions just came and people stopped me on the street and asked me how they could start their own business. Of course not! I have put huge amounts of effort into creating my business and expanding my area, but it has never been work to me. Of course I have had setbacks and challenges, but I have had joys and triumphs at the same time. My business has been a lot like raising my children. Anyone who has children can understand that there are trying times, but the joys outweigh those times so overwhelmingly that any effort is a labor of love. I would never call that work. With the milestones I have encountered with my children—watching them graduate from college, my daughter giving us two beautiful grandchildren, and my son taking up the entrepreneurial spirit and starting his own computer business—are mirrored to a lesser degree by seeing my dear friends, Karlee Isenhart and Linda Mcbroom, blossom into Independent National Sales Directors; seeing Kim Cavarretta build a dream home for her family when she once lived in mobile home with holes in the floors; and watching the evolution of my friends in the Philippines as they find hope for a prosperous future when it seemed so bleak. My Mary Kay business has not been my job; it has been my mission, my passion, and a part of my life and my family. I would wish that kind of work for everyone. Even as I no longer actively work my Mary Kay business, I know that whatever else I do, I will do because I love to do it. I believe in enriching the lives of others and I have devoted most of my life to just that. I am sure I will not stop. Even if I spend the rest of my life traveling with my children and grandchildren, I will love what I do and never work another day in my life.

Thank goodness God made us all different. We all have different talents, dreams, and things we love to do. After all, the world cannot be full of Mary Kay people or we would have no one to sell the product to. God has made us with talents as unique as our fingerprints; using those talents is what comes natural for us. That is why the idea of sitting on top of a rocket and being blasted into space is the biggest dream in the world for some and yet the last thing on earth others would want to do. To me that doesn't sound like very much fun, but I would imagine if you asked Neil Armstrong what he thought, it would be a different story. Sometimes I watch the guys that take care of our landscaping. I used to think of how sorry I felt for them working in the hot sun day in and day out until I spoke to them about it. They genuinely love what they do. They love being outside. The idea of sitting inside on the phone all day would drain the life out of them. They are their own bosses and they are wonderful at what they do. I could only imagine what the yard would look like if I had to do it; believe me it wouldn't look as good as they make it look. To me that would be work! But they have created a nice life for themselves and are very successful doing what they love.

When Steve Mariucci was the coach for the San Francisco 49ers football team, I remember watching him during pre-game warm-ups on television. One of the sound clips they played was of him watching his quarterback throw the ball to his teammates on a beautiful, warm day. He looked around at the fans who were filling in the seats and at the field, and he was so excited about what he was doing he walked over to one of the other coaches and said, "Gosh! I would do this for free!" That is loving what you do. That is having passion for your work and believing in your organization. Mary Kay also told us, "Find something you love to do so much that you would do it for free and someone will pay you a lot of money to do it." To give as many women the opportunity to secure their future and enrich their lives as I have been blessed to do and to see the smiles on the faces of women whose lives have been changed by something I have said or done gives me the satisfaction of knowing that I would do it all again—for free.

Find your passion, find your purpose. God has given you the seeds of greatness and the talents to achieve that greatness. The saddest thing would be to look back on you life and say, "What if I had tried?"

Get Your Systems in Place

Make your life easier. That sounds good, doesn't it? Well, for any person who owns his or her own business, you have to think about how to make your life easier. It is said that people will work eighty hours a week for themselves so they don't have to work forty hours a week for someone else. When you own your own business, it becomes part of your life and integrates with how you run your house and how you raise your children. The best thing you can do is make your life easier.

When I was on stage at Seminar in 1983 as the Sales Director with the number two unit in my seminar, I was asked to give a speech. I gave my speech, and I was more nervous about finishing my speech than I was about giving it. Back then, Mary Kay sat on the side of the stage and listened to the speeches; when the speaker finished, Mary Kay would call her over to tell her what a great job she had done. I finished my speech and I made my way off stage. Mary Kay met me with a hug and told me that she loved my speech, and that she knew I would come back the next year as the number one Sales Director at our Seminar. I was flattered of course by the sentiment and the confidence she had in me, but I had really devoted a lot of time to my business and had done all I thought I could do only to end up number two. So I looked at Mary Kay and asked how. She looked at me and said, "Anything that doesn't get you closer to your goal, don't do it. You can't spend dollar time on penny work." Then she explained to me that I had to get my systems in place so I could focus on what made the biggest difference in my business. My unit would not grow while I was doing laundry or scrubbing the floors, or even when I was making copies or mailing newsletters to the people in my unit. Those were all things that had to be done, but she made me realize that I didn't have to be the one to do them! I went home and immediately began getting more help. I got someone to clean the house, I got more help in my office and more help with the children. I didn't exactly know how I was going to pay for all this extra help, but I chose to take Mary Kay's advice. What a difference it made! I was able to utilize the time I had been spending on busy work; I spent this "new time" on developing and helping the people in my unit I was able to get more recruits, sell more product, hold more events, and even spend more time with my children. The best part about it was I made a lot more money! Even after I paid the new people around me, I had more money. I had more money, more time, and more business—my business was growing faster than ever. I had always heard that you have to spend money to make money, but I didn't learn it until that year. I returned to Seminar the following year as the number one Sales Director and debuted as an Independent National Sales Director thanks to the advice of Mary Kay and the systems I put in place.

Systems are people or organizational tools that make your life easier by automating things that have to be done. I know that to keep my house the way I like it I have to have it cleaned twice a week. So I know on Tuesdays and Thursdays my doorbell will ring, and whether I am there or not a lady will come in and clean my house. I also know that once a week the yard will be taken care of, and if anyone calls my house during a weekday, I know the phone will get answered and my emails will be checked, if I am there or not. It is a wonderful feeling to come home—from sharing Mary Kay halfway around the world for nearly a month—and pull into the driveway, tired and jetlagged, and see a beautifully manicured lawn, walk in to a clean house, crawl into fresh linens, and go to sleep without wondering if the mailbox is overflowing with mail or if my inbox is full. Having your systems in place gives you the freedom to work whenever you want to without having to worry if the little things are getting done.

The first systems I recommend people put in place are housekeeping and office help. Many women feel that it is their responsibility to maintain the house even if they have a full time business. What you must realize is that the number of hours in a week is set. You can do nothing to add more hours in your day, week, month, or year. Every hour you spend mopping the floor is one hour you cannot fully devote to anything else. If you try to multi-task, you end up with a half-cleaned floor and a half-listened to phone call, or whatever it was you were trying to pair it with. I have prioritized my life. I have my faith first, my family second, and my career third. If I had to continue with the list, I can assure you that mopping the floor would probably not make it in the top one hundred. So if I were to take an hour to mop my floor that is an hour that I have to take away from the top three priorities, and I am not willing to make that sacrifice. Instead I can delegate that to someone who is much more efficient at it than I am, likes to do it more than I do, and appreciates being paid well to do it for me. Everybody wins!

One of the best illustrations I have personally seen of how systems and priorities worked together happened to my daughter and son-in-law a few years ago. My son-in-law Chad graduated with a master's degree in Business Management and took a job with a large financial advisory firm. My daughter would have preferred for him to stay at home and help her, but he wanted to see where his path would take him. Along with being a financial advisor, he was still a coach for my grandson's football team. They have always prioritized their life the same way—faith first, family second, and career third. Chad was doing well with the financial firm but he was working long hours. When football season came around, he began going into the office at 6:30 in the morning and working through lunch so he could get all of his work done and leave at 5:30, just so he could get Jacob to football practice. A few weeks into the season, the manager called him into the office. He had noticed that Chad had been leaving the office while some of the other guys worked late. Chad explained that he was the first to come into the office in the mornings, he was the one that turned on the lights and opened the blinds and got to work. He was the one that worked through lunch. Since the financial markets close at 4:00 p.m., he was finished and had already spent an eleven-hour day by the time he left to take Jacob to football practice. The manager told Chad that, since he was the newest advisor, if other people were working late, he should be also. He continued to tell Chad that football is just a game and he needed to reexamine his priorities. Chad told him he would. He returned to his manager's office ten minutes later with his resignation. Chad called my daughter on the way home and asked if there were any positions available with her business. With Chad helping out with the kids, the house, and helping her in her office full time, doing all of the things that kept Pam and her assistant from focusing 100% on the business, Pam has become a Independent National Sales Director. They have more than doubled their income, more than replacing what he was making as a financial advisor. Chad has never missed a practice.

Power Up

Roger Bannister, Chris Brasher, and Christopher Chataway worked as a team. I have also talked to countless other athletes throughout the years and some of the most successful events they have had is when they have had a partner with which to run—someone that pushes them to do their best, helps them through the moments of weakness, and expects the same in return. I learned a lot from these athletes. When people form those kinds of relationships, these power partners as I like to call them, it seems that they both can accomplish more than either could have on their own. I have also found that it is more fun to run a race with a group. Even though I am not a runner, I have run my business much the same way. I have surrounded myself with people who charge after their goals with the same zest and determination that I do. We have fed off each other's energy the whole journey. My power partners have always been Karlee Isenhart and Linda McBroom. We have always pushed each other to accomplish more and to set our goals higher, then push even more in order to meet those goals. We have also celebrated our accomplishments together and relaxed together. Linda and Karlee are my power partners, and I dare to say that we have all accomplished more together than any of us could have on our own.

I encourage people to find power partners in every type of business they choose to pursue. Power partners give you an extra set of eyes to view challenges, an extra set of ears to hear ideas, and an extra set of hands to help with the "heavy lifting" that comes with hard work. The great thing about a power partner is that they are different from you. They see things a different way and have different ideas. They also have different emotions. Most of us know that life can be a roller coaster of emotion. We can be flying high one day and be down in the dumps the next. I have always found that my power partners can help smooth out the roller coaster by not letting me wallow in my "pity party" for too long, and by helping me pick myself up and keep on with the race. In turn, it has always been my job to come up with positive things to motivate Linda or Karlee when their wagon wasn't rolling well. We have laughed together, cried together, and had our ups and downs—but we always helped each other work through our stumbling blocks. The reason power partners work is because it is very rare that two people hit stumbling blocks at the same time. Just like in a race, if one partner is stumbling or falling behind, the other partner picks them up and helps them find their stride again. This might slow down the one who isn't stumbling for a little bit, but when the favor is returned down the road it all evens out and the team finishes stronger because of it.

The tricky thing about power partners is picking them.

1. You'll want to pick a power partner who shares your goals and ambition for success. Picking a power partner who has their sights set much lower than yours is less of a power partner and more of an anchor buddy. It would be like running a marathon with someone who is only running a 10K. Your team may get off to a strong start, but when your partner has reached their goal and you have helped them along the way, you have to either inspire them to passionately raise their expectations or go on alone with no one to help you if you falter. That is not why you picked a power partner in the first place.

2. You'll want to pick a power partner with a thick skin. You have to agree to hear criticisms along with the praises, and expect your partner to do the same—without it becoming personal. Your partner has to be able to tell you when you are slacking off or overreacting to a minor problem. That can be just as tough to say as it is to hear.

3. You'll want to be different. If you and your power partner are just alike then one of you isn't necessary. Differing personalities breed differing ideas and strategies. There are a million different routes to Chicago; the other person may know a better course than you. Different personalities handle stress and challenges differently. With all the different kinds of stress and challenges that can come to you, it is important to be able to help each other deal with

those challenges in a way the other partner may not see.

4. You'll want to be equal. With my power partners, Linda is, by virtue of the marketing plan, my off-spring, and Karlee is hers. But in our dynamic—as power partners—we are completely equal. Every idea is treated with the same respect and considered as thoroughly as any other, regardless of whose idea it is. At the same time we are all expected to carry our share of the burden. When it comes time to let our hair down, we all have the most fun. We have sheltered each other through life's storms and cel-ebrated in each other's accomplishments and bless-ings without regard to ranking or seniority. I can assure you that we have all benefited from our part-nership and our friendship more than we will ever know. I wish power partners like Linda and Karlee for every person who wants to be successful.

5. You and your power partner should be loyal. Working relationships can be as personal and volatile as any, and you can learn a lot about a person's personality and personal life when you work closely together. Because of the familiarity that can come from such a close and often intense relationship, it is important that you can trust one another with your dreams, aspirations, insecurities, and failures without wor-rying that such trust will be betrayed to others in the organization or used to hurt you or your partner

in any way. Betrayal of trust can doom any power partnership like it can just about any partnership, and all parties concerned will suffer major setbacks as a result.

6. With this, partnership there should be give and take. An uneven partnership is like bicycle with no wheels—it won't get very far. If you take from a partnership and use the support and advice when you need it, but are unavailable to give help in return, you stop assisting as a partner and instead become a parasite. People get rid of parasites quickly. To have a good power partner you have to be a good power partner.

Do It the Right Way Every Time

On an individual level, it is said that integrity is doing the right thing even when nobody is looking. As business people, it is hard to watch the news and see prime examples of integrity in business. What grabs the headlines are scandals and tales of multimillionaires stealing from the companies they are entrusted to run, lining their pockets with more than just their exuberant salaries and seemingly limitless perks. Surely, these scoundrels didn't wake up one morning and decide they would start pilfering the company pension fund, or bilking money to pay for extravagant parties on exotic islands. More than likely these people began cutting corners a long time ago. I'm sure they weren't trained to steal or deceive, but they learned to advance by manipulating the system little by little and doing things "just a little wrong." As these indiscretions led to seemingly better performances and no one seemed to get hurt, the indiscretions grew unchecked by those who failed to look or did not want to see. In a business with Mary Kay, we are independent contractors. We are the CEO and the board of directors all rolled into one. We are in charge of running our businesses, and we are also solely responsible for the consequences of how we run it. My advice is to run your business as if Mary Kay Ash were standing beside you, watching every phone call you make and every class you hold. Cutting corners is a very slippery slope that might offer very short-term rewards, but will ultimately lead your business to ruin, along with your reputation. Worse, you can damage the reputation of your sister Beauty Consultants, Sales Directors, and all those who have come before you. You can tarnish the memory of Mary Kay Ash through dishonest business practices. Mary Kay told us, "Honesty is the cornerstone of all success, without which confidence and the ability to perform shall cease to exist." As the CEO and board of directors of your business, you are allowed a lot of freedom; ultimately you are also solely accountable for how your business is run. Mary Kay Inc. has flourished because the Independent Beauty Consultants, Sales Directors, and National Sales Directors have been honest and respected members of their business communities and have worked very hard to further uplift the reputation of the Company as one built on honesty, fairness, and compassion. I believe this lesson is one that translates to all businesses. I believe that businesses that are run ethically, practice charity, and benefit the community are often times more successful because people feel good about giving them business. But even if practicing morality and ethics don't translate into a significant increase in sales, the reward is in the piece of mind that you are doing the right thing. It is much easier for me to rest my head at night knowing that I acted in the best interest of my customers, my area, and my business. There is peace in knowing that by following the godly principle of "do unto others as you would have them do onto you," you free yourself of the burden of being caught doing something wrong! I cannot imagine the CEOs, who have recently been accused of numerous scandals, slept well at night without the fear of their misdeeds being exposed. I feel confident that, more often than not, the light eventually shines on the indiscretions of the unjust. And once a trust for your business has been lost, it is so hard if not impossible to rebuild. If each one of us strives to do business the right way every time and teach other people to do the same, we can be proud to be affiliated with such outstanding companies for decades to come.

Dress for Success

When I was first starting out in my Mary Kay business, I was told to imagine everyday before I left my house that Mary Kay herself was standing on my front porch to see how I looked. I know that seems a little extreme, but what I learned is that when you are your own boss you never know when a business opportunity will come your way. I never wanted to be at the grocery store and meet a sharp lady and feel as if I wasn't dressed well enough to talk to her about my business. What I found, however, is that when you take the time to make yourself look professional, people want to know where you're going or what you do. I can't count the amount of times I was at the store and another lady in line said, "Don't you look nice, are you going somewhere?" That was always the perfect opportunity to tell them all about my Mary Kay business; I could ask them if they would like to hold a class or attend a guest event. Another thing I know is that when you know you look professional and well put together, it gives you confidence. You walk taller, you smile more, and you have an air about you that tells people you are successful. Even if you are just starting out you can dress in a way that makes people notice that you take your business seriously. An old saying sums it up well. "Clothes make the man." That was obviously coined before women were prominent in the workplace, but in generic terms, rings true. For most people what they put on can change the way they feel. Putting on a nice dress, which you know enhances your positives and downplays your negatives, on your anniversary can make you feel more romantic; for a man to put on a tuxedo may cause him to act more refined and gentlemanly. I firmly believe that the kind of person who is attracted to you is the kind of person you are. So if you want to attract sharp, well-put together people then you should start by being that kind of person.

My longtime friend and sister Independent National Sales Director Scarlett Walker exemplifies the motto "dress for success" as well as anyone I have ever met. She always looks perfect. When she enters a room, people notice her; they want to know who she is and what she does. She is automatically recognized as a woman of taste and elegance. I believe she is probably the most put together person anywhere she goes. As a result, when she talks to women about a business opportunity they usually want to listen. People inherently grant a certain amount of authority to sharply dressed people. This happens for the same reason real estate agents tend to drive nice cars. People naturally assume that if you drive a nice car then you make a lot of money. If you make a lot of money then you must be good at what you do, and if you are good at what you do then you must know what you are talking about when it comes to that subject. So if they want to know more about that subject, be it real estate or cosmetics, people are more willing to give their attention to the people they presume to be successful. When Scarlett enters a room dressed well, and has taken the time to make sure she presents herself well, then people tend to give her more of their attention and are more willing to follow her as a leader.

The same is true for you. Ask yourself, *If I needed advice on a major career change or a major life event and I happen to meet someone who claimed to have the answers I was looking for but looked like they just rolled out of bed, how seriously would I take that advice?* If I need someone to tell me what is wrong with my car, I trust a person with a little grease on his hands. If I need a leader, I am looking for someone who is dressed like they are on their way to the top. Why would I follow someone who can't even dress the part? I have always believed in dressing for success. Mary Kay asked that we dress professionally and conservatively because she felt that she wanted people to see us as professionals and our Mary Kay business as a serious business opportunity; after all we only get one chance to make a first impression. If men were going to put on suits to go to work at IBM then why shouldn't the independent sales force dress professionally to represent Mary Kay Inc.? Mary Kay actually reinforced this belief by establishing an Independent Sales Directors' suit and an Independent National Sales Directors' suit that could be worn by the ladies who were advancing up the ladder of success. Both of these suits change yearly for the most part, and have always been professional and stylish at the same time. The women who wear these suits realize that they represent success and advancement, and for the most part they exude that successful air to those around them.

Unfortunately, we live in a society that judges us by our appearance. Even though I teach in this book that we should not pre-judge anyone based on what is on the outside, not everyone has learned this lesson. In our world, people decide rather quickly if they believe a person they have met is worthy of being a leader or a mentor to them; one of the ways they decide this is by the image that person projects to them. When you go out during the day, what image do you project? Is it an image that warrants respect and professionalism? When I think of image I often think of the movie *Pretty Woman* starring Julia Roberts. One of my favorite scenes in the movie is when her character is shopping in the posh, upscale stores with plenty of money to buy whatever she wants. The store attendants won't wait on her because she is not dressed like their normal clientele. With a few new outfits and a hair appointment, she is no longer shunned by the store clerks. Instead, people fall over themselves to help her with whatever she needs. After the makeover, she walks with confidence, acting as if she deserves to be in any shop on the street. Her new appearance commands more respect and attention. Of course, the scene from the movie is a dramatic example and quite a transformation, but the lesson is still there and can be seen played out in stores and businesses everyday. What a shame it would be for someone to miss the wonderful leader inside you and the wonderful gifts you have to offer because you were too busy to take the time to make yourself look as professional as possible.

Work with Discipline

Working with discipline is mainly for those who are self-employed or work from home. The reason for this is that if you go into an office or report to a manager everyday, you probably have someone else creating that discipline for you. If you don't work when you should for a boss then that usually shows pretty quickly and resolves itself. Either your boss motivates you to work when you should, or you will probably be looking for a new boss at another job to motivate you. But working on your own is a completely different animal. You have the freedom to set your hours, arrange your priorities, or to slack off whenever you want. The freedom can be its own challenge. How we handle that freedom can determine our successes or our failures.

I wrote earlier of my dear friend and offspring National Sales Director Carol Robertson. It is only right that I dedicate this chapter to her because she personified what it meant to work with discipline. I think besides the phrase, "I love you," it may have been what she said the most. Carol was a top Sales Director for several years, always had the most beautiful smile on her face and a kind word for anyone she met. But her positive attitude and effervescent personality was not a result of a carefree life where everything fell into place just as she had planned. She was upbeat in spite of the fact that she had marital trouble, which left her raising two small children on her own. The experience would have been enough for many to pack it in and give up on hopes and dreams, but Carol's troubles forged her into one of the most disciplined people I have ever met. She told people all the time, "Work hard during the good times and that foundation will carry you through the bad times." Carol also lived what she taught and she worked with great discipline, which propelled her business to grow fantastically. Eventually, she met the man that she always called the love of her life, Brian Robertson. They dated, fell in love, and were married. Some women would use a new love, a new marriage, and eventually a beautiful baby girl to distract them from working, and put their businesses on hold. Carol was exactly the opposite. She used the energy from her lifestyle to propel her business in high gear. She climbed the ladder of success with Mary Kay, and shared her joy for life and her business with practically everyone she met. Then just as she was about to enter her qualification to become an Independent National Sales Director, the pinnacle of success in Mary Kay, she and Brian learned that he was going to battle cancer. Anyone that knew Carol also knew that he would not be fighting alone. Carol was by his side every moment, giving him the love, strength, and encouragement he needed to get him through his grueling ordeal. But because she had worked so diligently during the good times, the people in her area knew exactly what to do. They pulled together and not only sustained their business but excelled. They supported her and helped her achieve her Independent National Sales Director Qualification! Her philosophy of working with discipline came full circle to help carry her through a very dark time in her life, teaching a very valuable lesson to everyone around her. As I mentioned earlier, even though Brian seemed to make a full recovery and was able to attend Carol's National Sales Director debut, he eventually lost his battle with cancer. Less than a year later, a terrible accident took Carol from us. As tragic as her loss has been for all of us, and as terribly saddened as we all are that we will never be graced by her insurmountable positivism in this life, she is a role model, truly living those words she spoke so many times. We lost Carol one day before her second anniversary of becoming a National Sales Director. If she had waited just one year while Brian was battling his cancer, we would have all understood—but that is not how she lived her life. The success she achieved has helped to provide for her three children since she has passed. In their honor I would like to pass on to you the advice that she personified for all of us, "Work with discipline, not emotion. Work during the good times and it will carry you through the bad times." My close friend Shirley Oppenheimer, who is also an Independent Senior National Sales Director, has also taught me the definition of discipline. From the moment Shirley began her Mary Kay business, she was a superstar. She worked hard and diligently under the guidance of and with her Independent Senior Sales Director, Johnnette Shealy, from the very beginning. Shirley worked with discipline everyday because she knew she and her family wanted more and needed more in their life; Shirley's work ethic opened the doors for that to happen. From those humble beginnings as personnel manager at Altus Air Force Base in Oklahoma, Shirley has worked her way to become a dynamic, successful leader of leaders as an Independent Senior National Sales Director. Shirley also learned the value of working with discipline when a few years ago she was diagnosed with breast cancer. With the support of her loving family and her fantastic area she was able withstand the fourteen surgeries it has taken to beat the dreaded disease. She still has a thriving business, which she was able to return to. Her outstanding discipline has changed her family's life—living paycheck to paycheck—to a celebration of life and abundance. Taking a cue from his wife, her work, and discipline, Shirley's husband, Cliff, was able to leave the Air Force, and become a highly successful entrepreneur in his own right.

Working with discipline is not only about working for fear of falling ill. It is more that we should all sow while the sun is shining because there may be rain in the future. We should be happy about the opportunities we have to improve our lives and take advantage of the great health and time we have. The times we need a break from our work can come from all kinds of sources, both good and bad. By not squandering the good days, working through the temptations to procrastinate, and not succumbing to creative avoidance, we have those days in the bank. Creative avoidance is the ability so many of us have to find a million other things to do except what we should be doing in that moment. I have seen people clean their entire house, organize their pantry, and rearrange all the closets instead of picking up the phone to call an upset customer or to book appointments. When we practice creative avoidance, we know that we should be working our business but we don't feel like we are procrastinating because we are doing something constructive. In reality you are just procrastinating in a cleaner house.

So if you are a procrastinator or you are an expert at creative avoidance, does that mean you are doomed to a life of mediocrity? Of course not! There are ways to overcome procrastination and create an environment where you become like Shirley or Carol, working with discipline everyday. The first thing you have to do is get out of bed. This seems like easy enough advice, but it is amazing what people will do when they no longer punch a clock for someone else and go to work for themselves. If you work for yourself or work from home you are the only one who can create your routine. Some people like to exercise to get the blood flowing in the morning, so if this is what you do then you have to allot time for that. That does not mean waking up at the crack of noon and then working out; much of the day is then gone, and if you have to run a few errands the day is gone, everyone else is coming home from school and work, and you get pulled in a thousand different directions. Today is the only one you get. When today is gone, it is gone forever and you cannot get that time back. Each day must be cherished for the gift that it is and the opportunity it gives us to move our dreams forward. So if you set your alarm clock for a decent time that gets you up and ready before noon then you have begun to create a routine. Mary Kay Ash used to challenge us to be a member of the 5:00 a.m. club because she said it would add so much productivity to our day we wouldn't believe it. As much as I have worked to follow every instruction she ever gave, I have never been a successful member of the 5:00 a.m. club. I know people who are and I applaud them. However, getting up is not enough. You'll want to get up and get dressed just like preparing for an office. When you dress like a businessperson you have a tendency to act more like a businessperson.

Another thing you will want to do is define your workspace. John Maxwell says that we should take time everyday to spend personal quiet time with ourselves—praying, meditating, or just thinking about where we would like to see our day and our life take us. He has even designated a special place in his home just for this time. He calls it his "thinking chair." The only time he sits in that chair is when he is thinking. He doesn't stop and sit down in it when he needs to tie his shoe, he doesn't watch television from it, he doesn't even take phone calls sitting in his thinking chair. As a result he has conditioned himself to be completely focused when he is in that chair. Because he is focused he can get his mind straight for the day and come out of the time in his thinking chair ready to meet the day head on. I understand there are very few John Maxwells in the world, and that is what makes him so special; but what we can take from his example is that designating space can help you to be more productive. I believe that every person who works from home or for themselves should have a designated office space. Whether it is a spare bedroom converted to a home office or a commercial space you lease away from home, it is imperative that you have a space that is dedicated to getting work done. This means it does not double as a kitchen table, or your bedroom, or even your car. There needs to be one place, no matter how small, that you know when you sit down there you have one purpose—to go to work. In my house I have three floors. The entire downstairs of my home is my office, all two thousand square feet of it. It does not double as a game room or a media room, it is my office. When I walk down those stairs, it is to go to work and nothing else. I have conditioned myself that way since my office was a corner in an already cramped house, but that was my workspace and that was all it was.

When we mix our office in with the rest of our house, we have the tendency to not distinguish work time from house time, and then we find ourselves going to work as soon as the dishes are done, or the carpet is vacuumed, or "Oh my goodness are those dust bunnies under the sofa?" When you integrate your work and your life, life will sneak in front. Then you find yourself scrambling at the end of the month to get a whole lot of work done so the bills get paid. And when we scramble, that is when quality work gets tossed aside for quantity work, which is not what careers are built on. Or on the contrary, when there is not a separation between home life and work life, some people never get off work. Some people can never relax if their home and work are not separated because they feel like they are always at work. This deprives the person and their family of the mom, wife, and person they can be when they are off work. I have known people who get a planner and use different color markers to designate their schedule between work, housework, free time, spiritual time, and family time to ensure they have that balance in their life. As the old saying goes, all work and no play makes Jack a dull boy. The reason we strike out on our own is to create our lives exactly the way we want them to be, free from the constraints of the corporate world. When we work with discipline, we can be more efficient and more effective. Your life is the sum total of what you do every single day. If you work towards your goals and dreams everyday, you will get closer everyday. If you avoid your work then you have put off your dreams for one more day; too many of those and you may run out of days to reach your dreams.

Diversify Your Business

Because of the position I attained with Mary Kay Inc. and the events I have held, I have mingled with and brushed elbows with a lot of very successful men and women. As a result, I have found that successful people are always giving each other financial advice. "You need to invest in real estate," they say, or "I buy stocks when the market is trending upward and hedge my portfolio against the decline with bonds." I have talked to people who have advised me to have insurance and to buy art, gold, or diamonds in case the dollar loses its value. The reason people say I should do these things is for diversity. A financial advisor will tell you that the proper mix of investments will ensure that you always have something gaining value, even if one sector of the economy is going south. I guess it has all been decent advice, and I have protected myself as well as I can. But I don't think I ever needed someone with MBA or a CFP (certified financial planner) to give me that advice. Since I was five years old I have heard that you don't put your eggs in one basket. I also heard Mary Kay say, "Grow where you're planted." So I have taken both of these pieces of advice to heart and diversified my business whenever I could.

There are different ways to diversify. Some businesses diversify by selling different types of products like gas grills and propane heaters. They sell gas grills because they sell well in the summer and propane heaters for the winter. Other businesses diversify geographically. If you go to almost any mutual fund website or financial planner, you can buy mutual funds that are whole groups of companies put together; when you buy that mutual fund you get a little piece of stock in those companies. One of the ways they group mutual finds are domestic and international. If you buy both kinds you are really diversifying. First, you are buying little shares in a whole lot of companies, and the odds of all of those companies doing badly at the same time are pretty small. Secondly, you are diversifying geographically. You are not only buying little shares of a lot of companies in the United States, but you are also buying little shares of companies all over the world. So the odds that something can happen to affect the United States, Europe, and China all at the same time—causing all of your mutual funds to go down—is pretty small. While building my business, I diversified geographically. I made a conscious effort to expand my area every time we moved and even every time we visited somewhere else. To take it a step farther, I actively chose to expand my area to foreign countries. I had consultants in nearly every state in the United States as well as in Canada, Mexico, Malaysia, Korea, and the Philippines. I even made sure that Consultants who moved away stayed connected so they could grow a whole new area. Of course this meant I traveled a lot, but I love to travel. As a result I could rest a little easier knowing that, even though there may be a blizzard in the Midwest and some of the people in my area who lived there would not be able to hold as many classes or attend events that week, people in my area who didn't live in the Midwest could do business as usual. I have always encouraged the Consultants and Sales directors in my area to diversify their businesses as well because it can provide a larger support group for everyone if one area has a problem. I remember when Hurricane Katrina hit the Gulf Coast of the United States. That was a devastating and terrifying time for all of us. So many people in my area were affected including Independent National Sales Directors Vicky Fuselier, who lives in Lake Charles, Louisiana, and Scarlett Walker, who lives in Plano, Texas (but has a group of Consultants in Houma, Louisiana). Their lives and businesses were completely turned upside down. But because there were so many of us who were not directly affected, we were able to help them, care for them, love them, and help them get their lives and businesses back on track.

I have been proud that so many people associated with me in my Mary Kay business have also diversified their businesses as well. My dear friend, Senior National Sales Director Linda McBroom, has part of her area in Korea. My daughter, Pam, has helped open Mary Kay in Malaysia, the Philippines, Thailand, and India, and plans to keep on traveling, sharing the Mary Kay opportunity with women all over the world. So many more have caught the vision of diversifying their business all over the country and the world, and are loving every minute of it. They are helping to secure their futures while enriching the lives of others everywhere they go.

Be a Good Steward of Your Business

You are the face of your business. Whatever business it is that you are involved in, you are who is associated as the face of your business. You may have never thought of it that way, but it can really change some of your decisions on a daily basis when you do. To some people you may be the only person from whatever company you work for that they will ever meet. Because that is often the case, these people can only assume that everyone in the company is just like you.

In Mary Kay we talk a lot about image. Is the image the sales force is presenting a favorable representation of who we are? We ask people to always dress professionally when they are doing their Mary Kay business. If you are the face of Mary Kay Inc. when you are out in your town, it is in your best interest for your business and the Company if you look professional and well put together. How you look and act translates to what people think of the Company. If you work as a lawyer at a local firm and every time people see you you're shabbily or provocatively dressed with your hair a mess, what do you think people will think about the firm you represent? People may assume that if you are not professional then the company you represent is not professional. When it comes to business, people want professionalism. On the other hand, what do people think if every time they see you, you are well dressed with your hair and makeup perfect? They probably think that is a company that has sharp people. Better yet what do people think when they see you at all the charity events, or on the local news for heading fundraisers for those in need? Not only do they think that you are a good person, they also think you are someone they would like to be associated with.

Two women with whom I have been proud to be associated for many, many years, Kim Cavarretta and Debbie Elbrecht, are Independent Sales Directors who are not only great friends, but they are incredible stewards of their businesses. They represent themselves and Mary Kay Inc. wonderfully everywhere they go. It comes easily to Kim and Debbie because they are genuinely wonderful people; but they also go the extra mile to ensure that they are always a positive image for Mary Kay Inc. . They volunteer in the community and organize wonderful charitable events like Mary Kay Day at the ballpark. They have organized, with the St. Louis Cardinals, charity fundraising by bringing Mary Kay families and staff to the St. Louis Cardinals ballpark to raise money for the Mary Kay Ash Charitable Foundation. Kim and Debbie, along with hundreds of Mary Kay Independent Beauty Consultants, Sales Directors, and their families, go to the ballpark en masse to raise money and awareness for cancers that affect women as well as domestic violence. The team allows the ladies to drive around the field in their Mary Kay pink Cadillacs and show their support for the foundation. They have raised a great deal of money during the years doing fundraisers like the St. Louis Cardinals Mary Kay Day; at the same time they have shown the people of the community that they are people who give of themselves to help others.

Being a good steward of your business is all about showing others that you are a valuable member of the community, and that your business has a symbiotic relationship with the community (in that both your business and the community benefit from your business being there). Volunteering your time as a coach to a local team or taking meals to the elderly who can't get out on their own are examples of not only being a good steward of your business, but being a good person. When you are a good person, giving of yourself, your community benefits and your business benefits, but you are the one who benefits the most. Winston Churchill, the Prime Minister of the United Kingdom during World War II and a wonderful orator, said it best when he said, "We make a living by what we get, we make a life by what we give."

A Family Affair

Any time you own your own business it directly affects your family and my Mary Kay Business truly became a family affair. The key is to make the effects of the business on your family positive ones. I found it was very important to get the entire family involved and to let them know what my goals were. I have always let my children know how we were doing and the progress we were making. Once I became an Independent National Sales Director, I always took my children to seminars so they could share in the recognition. I wanted to be a role model for the people in my organization, so when they would ask me how to get family involvement I could give them specific examples. As for my children, I always got them involved in the business. I would talk to them about people who were moving up, introducing them to anyone that came to our home for Mary Kay functions. I wanted them to know who I was building my business with so they would have an interest in how well everyone did.

Many of the ladies in our area have become like family members themselves and our children have grown up together.

These "family members"—Linda and Denny McBroom, along with their children, Courtney and Mike Flynn; Chris and Karen Cole; and Karlee and Jerry Isenhart, with their children, Bryce, Bryan and his wife Jennifer—travel and vacation with us, go to each other's weddings, and share all of the events as a family would. This has given us a bond that gives everyone a reason to care about how the business is doing. It also invites friendly competition between us, which pushes us to excel. Furthermore, between us, all of our daughters and daughters-in law have their own Mary Kay businesses. How much does that say when it thrills a mother to have her daughter do what she does. People used to say, "I work like I do so my children won't have to." In our lives, we are so happy that we get to share this opportunity with our family. Pam didn't jump at the chance to become an Independent Beauty Consultant as soon as she turned eighteen. She went to college and studied pre-law in hopes of going to law school, but during her senior year she got a job with a telemarketing firm and quickly moved into management; she saw how hard these people worked and how little they got paid. I think that, coupled with her not being thrilled with the idea of more school right after she graduated, made her reconsider. She called me one day and told me she wanted me to help her start her own Mary Kay business. I was thrilled, but I also knew why she hesitated. She knew that everyone would be watching her because she is my daughter. She was terrified of failing and what all of these people she had known her whole life would think. But she overcame her fears and began working her business. I thought it was so funny when she told me that people would ask her questions about Mary Kay and she would answer them without missing a beat, then think to herself in a few minutes, *How did I know to say that?* It was from all of the years of hearing me talk to people and educate people, and I didn't think she was listening! Pam and I became the fifth mother and daughter to both reach the position of Independent National Sales Director in the history of the company; my great friend Shirley Oppenheimer and her daughter, Terri Schafer, have since become the sixth mother and daughter to reach the same goal.

We are also proud to announce that the third mother and daughter Independent National Sales Directors are also from our Fortenberry Family—Scarlett Walker and Kimberly Copeland. It is certainly a Family affair!

It's been one of the great joys of my life to watch them become Independent National Sales Directors, and I am so proud of them.

I believe married women that go into business for themselves do better if they can get their husbands involved. Mary Kay said, "You can do your business with a husband or without a husband; just not against a husband." So in my area, we have a vested interest in garnering a husband's support for his wife's business. My husband loves to play golf, so when we have big functions he organizes a golf outing for the guys and a husbands' class. Many times it is the reason the men come to an event for the first time. They learn that this is a real business and that with their support, their wives can move up faster in the business. We have heard story after story of men, unsupportive of their wives' businesses, who come to a golf outing or a husbands' class and are completely turned around, becoming champions of their wife's business. Once a husband is involved he can become an excellent motivator for his wife. When I was a brand new Consultant in O'Fallon, Illinois, I took Charles to a potluck dinner at Miriam Alexander's home (it always seems easier to get men to come to a function when there is golf or food involved). At Miriam's home, after dinner, she recognized the consultants by presenting them with ribbons and prizes and unfortunately I didn't receive any. I will never forget on the ride home, Charles asked me, "Why didn't you receive any recognition?" He wasn't being critical or mean spirited; he was just wondering. I vowed then and there that I would never miss another chance for recognition, especially when Charles was coming. He motivated me with that one comment for the next twenty-five years.

The funny thing I have learned about women is that, many times, they will do things for their husbands and children that they will not do for themselves. A woman will work harder to earn the money to get her child braces than she will to buy something she wants. Women will make the extra phone call or talk to one more stranger to get closer to a goal if it is for recognition their husbands can see. They sometimes may work harder for the joy of sharing the goal with others than they will just for themselves. We love to provide for our families and we love for our loved ones to be proud of us. That is why I have always encouraged women to bring their husbands to any function we have. That is also why Charles began to travel everywhere with me once he retired. He does a great job of getting the husbands involved in their wives' businesses. He talks to them about taxes and how they can help. But mainly I believe that these husbands look at Charles and say to themselves, *If it is okay for a retired combat pilot and Colonel in the United States Air Force to help his wife then I can certainly help mine.* I also believe that the husbands have such a good time together that it encourages their wives not to miss functions and to qualify for everything their husbands can attend.

We sometimes wonder why the husbands aren't supportive right from the beginning, but it is not that hard to see. What if your husband or significant other withdrew $1,000 to start an in-home business, then started leaving a couple nights a week to hang out with a bunch of other guys? Would it matter if he came home really excited and positive, if you never saw at least that $1,000 go back into the bank? The one thing that usually will turn around an unsupportive husband is income. As Jerry Maguire would say, "Show me the money!" Most men can get excited about their wife dressing up more, being more excited about her day, having a more positive attitude, and putting extra money into the family account. Most of the time the first three on that list would just be a bonus! The best part is when you start making money and buying extra things for the family or paying off some bills; your husband will get more excited and will help free up your schedule so you can work your business. He will tell his friends at work and maybe get their wives interested. After all, I got recruited through Charles, and having someone like me in your business can really be a good thing.

I have had a wonderful journey since I left my tiny hometown in Mississippi. In some ways I am still the same woman who made Baked Alaska in 4H Club, played basketball, and married my high school sweetheart. But in other ways I know

I have grown—as a person, as a woman, and as a leader. I have listened to anyone that would teach me how to be a better communicator, mentor, friend, and businesswoman. Even though the majority of my working life I have been in the beauty business, my life has been so much more than makeup. I have dedicated myself to finding my inner strength and uncovering the leader God planted inside me. I have also dedicated my life to passing on these lessons. I know none of us will ever get it perfect, but I will never stop striving towards some semblance of perfection. I realize that it is the journey that makes us who we are and our only legacy is those that are influenced and inspired by us. But the few things I have learned that seem to encompass all the other details are simple rules of life that I have chosen to live and work by. I know they make all the difference.

Try your hardest to always do what you know in your heart is the right thing, regardless of what it means to the "bottom line."

Imagine everyone you meet has a sign around his or her neck that says, "Make me feel important."

And finally and most importantly—

Give yourself and everyone you meet unconditional love.

> Master, which is the great commandment in the law?
> Jesus said unto him, Thou shalt love the Lord thy God with all thy heart, and with all thy soul, and with all thy mind.
> This is the first and great commandment.
> And the second is like unto it, Thou shalt love thy neighbour as thyself.
>
> Matthew 22:36–39

My Friend, Mary Kay Ash

Since I have been involved with Mary Kay Inc. for more than thirty-two years, I have had the honor and privilege to know and befriend Mary Kay Ash. When I became an Independent Beauty Consultant in 1975, the Company was small; however, it always seemed big to me. There was only one Seminar in 1976, but it was just like the five the Company has today. Everything was first class and ran like clockwork. There was the same beautiful "million-dollar" stage and Mary Kay Ash stood on the stage and gave away diamonds, diamond bar pins, and fur coats. She made every person who came across that stage feel important. I remember sitting at my first seminar looking up there and seeing Mary Kay as she hugged those winners like they were her own family. I sat there with a dream in my heart that one day I would be on that stage, and get the chance to hug Mary Kay myself. Luckily, I got my chance to spend time with Mary Kay before she passed away, but I would be so happy to have just a little more. For those people who never got the chance to know what a genuine and wonderful person Mary Kay Ash was, this book will close with some personal stories of my relationship with Mary Kay.

Mary Kay Ash was truly a remarkable woman. She was smart, funny, and every bit as warm as she comes across in video clips and stories. What I think I loved about her most, though, is that she was a genuinely down-to-earth person. I remember one time I stopped by her office to talk to her about something and as we spoke, she began to tell me about the beautiful new pink house she had just moved into. She told me her only concern with the house was that she had noticed that her electric and water bills were so much higher in the new house than they were in the old house. She believed that she really needed to get the utility companies to come out and check that everything was okay with the house. Here she was, the head of a multimillion-dollar company, and she wanted to be sure she wasn't wasting a few hundred dollars a month in water or electricity. That was so like her. She clipped coupons for the grocery store until she had her stroke. With the stories we are constantly hearing about corporate waste and the exorbitant spending of CEOs, it was—and still is!—refreshing to know that at least one company was founded by a woman who saw the value of clipping a coupon.

I am so very grateful that I started my business and grew in my business so I could be mentored by and spend time with Mary Kay. Once I learned how to be a leader and grew my business, I was able to call and talk to Mary Kay. I will always be grateful for Erma Thompson, Mary Kay's personal assistant; she always put me right through to Mary Kay if she was in and let me talk to my mentor. Mary Kay took my calls even when I wasn't an Independent National Sales Director, but a top Independent Sales Director, because I didn't have a mentor—Mary Kay filled that roll for me. Early in my business when I lived in O'Fallon, Illinois, I was having some challenges and needed some advice. There was to be a Jamboree in St. Louis and Mary Kay was going to be there. I called Erma and set up some personal time with Mary Kay in her suite. As soon as I arrived in Mary Kay's suite, she immediately began asking me questions about my family, my unit, and my future area. She was genuinely concerned about each aspect of my life and made me feel like I was the only sales person in the whole company. That is one thing that always struck me about her. Mary Kay Ash could always make you feel like you were the only person that mattered when you were talking to her. It was like the building could crumble around you and she wouldn't even notice because she was so focused on her conversation with you. She didn't just preach to make others feel special, she lived it. I soon realized that I didn't even talk to her about my challenges; they just seemed to melt away. She always had the right words to make me feel special, important, and like I could accomplish anything. I left her suite that night knowing that I would be an Independent National Sales Director.

A few years later, in 1979, I had moved to Las Vegas. As I was getting dressed one morning, the phone rang. I answered and the voice on the other end said, "Good morning, how are you?" One of the things Mary Kay taught me was that when anyone asked me how I was doing the only thing that should come out of my mouth should be, "Great," not "okay" or "fine" but "Great!" So I answered, "Great!" Then the voice on the other end said, "Can you guess who this is?" and I answered, "I don't know." When I realized it was Mary Kay, I was so glad I had answered the way she had taught me. She was in Las Vegas to see a few of the shows to get some ideas for themes for seminar. The night before she went to see the Liberace show. After the show, she was invited backstage to meet the flamboyant showman himself. As a gift, Mary Kay decided to present Liberace with a complete line of skin care products. In addition, she told him that she would send one of her top people to deliver the products and show him how to use them. That's why she called me. Long story short, I spent a lot of time in Liberace's home (more time with his housekeeper than him actually), and was finally able to present him with the products. The most exciting part of the experience was not meeting Liberace or seeing his home, which was quite lavish; it was that fact that Mary Kay thought enough to select me and call me personally. Again, she made me feel so special and so loved.

When we lived in Abilene, Texas, in the early 80s, we planned a trip to Mississippi to visit our families at Christmas time. We knew we would be driving through Dallas on our way home on December 28, so I called Erma and asked if I could bring my family to see Mary Kay's office. Erma was so gracious and set up the time. When we got there we were so surprised to find Mary Kay there, sitting behind her desk. She invited us in; we pulled up the chairs and she treated my family like they were her very own. She gave my daughter and my son autographed pictures. She gave them signed copies of her autobiography and posed for pictures with us that we still treasure to this day. Before we left that day she made Charles promise to wear his military uniform when I debuted as an Independent National Sales Director. She not only made us feel important, but she had taken me to the next level in my thinking. I knew I wanted to be an Independent National Sales Director but she talked about it as if it were already happening. I thought of it as something off in the distance; she brought my vision to something that was right around the corner. That is what a visionary does—she instilled her vision in me. In 1984 our unit was the number one unit at the Sapphire Seminar, and I debuted as an Independent National Sales Director. This was certainly a lesson well learned for me. She was always demonstrating what she taught us.

Just before Seminar in 1985, the President of Mary Kay Inc., Dick Barlett, called and asked if I would be on *Good Morning America* with Mary Kay Ash. I didn't have to think twice about it, I was so honored and excited. As the date approached, however, I have to admit I did begin to get a little nervous. Mary Kay had told me countless times, "What you think about, you bring about; both good and bad." So, I heeded her words and kept repeating to myself, *I am not nervous, I have no reason to be nervous.* And it worked ... mostly, until Dick called me back and told me that the show would be taped from our seminar stage in front of 7,000 people and broadcast to the rest of the country. He told me he would pick me up in front of my hotel about 7:30 in the morning so I could get my hair and make up done at the convention center where the seminar and the show would be held. I kept telling myself that there was nothing to be nervous about because I had been involved with Mary Kay Inc. for more than ten years, and I certainly knew the products and the company very well; and no matter what, I would have Mary Kay there beside me. When I arrived to get my make up done I was so relieved to see Mary Kay in the chair beside mine. She immediately made me feel better by talking about my family and my business, taking my mind off the show. The memory of chatting with Mary Kay as we had professionals doing our make up had to be the highlight of the whole day. When we were finished with our hair and make up it was show time. My nerves crept up on me again and by the time we were seated and the director shouted, "Action!" I was nervous. I tried to smile, but my mouth was dry and my lips stuck to my teeth. I looked over at Mary Kay and there she sat, like she was relaxing in her living room with all the poise of a movie star. As she smiled at me, I felt calm inside. I licked my teeth and had the time of my life on national television with Mary Kay Ash. She could lead without saying a word.

I will always remember my visits to Dallas to work with my friend and first line Independent Sales Director Libby Hopkins. I scheduled visits for us to go in and see Mary Kay in her office. It was always so exciting to just sit and talk to her even though we knew she could have been doing a million other things. She was after all the founder and owner of a multimillion-dollar company! She always made time for us, though. One time we were visiting with Mary Kay and she mentioned she was getting hungry; Libby told Mary Kay that she had just made a batch of tamales. We knew that Mary Kay loved Mexican food, so Libby asked her if she wanted us to bring her a plate of tamales. Mary Kay thought about it and said, "I hate to ever turn down tamales." So we went and made Mary Kay Ash a plate of tamales and took them to her like we were going to a potluck dinner. I am always amazed at how down to earth Mary Kay was, yet was still able to inspire and excited us. We always left her feeling like there wasn't a thing in the world we couldn't do.

Mary Kay didn't reserve her wisdom just for the ladies either. When Charles and I were in Canada for their Seminar in 1985, Charles was on his way from the hotel to teach a class of Mary Kay husbands when he ran into Mary Kay. Mary Kay offered Charles a ride in her limo to the convention center, and talked to Charles on the ride over. Finally, Charles asked Mary Kay, "What should I tell the men in the husbands' class?" Mary Kay said, "Tell them to pat their wife on the back, up high, everyday, and tell her you love her, and she will make you a rich man." Not only did Charles take that advice and pass it on to the husbands in the class, but he took it to heart himself and it has worked out just like she said it would.

One of the most exciting times in my business was when Mary Kay flew to Las Vegas to do a guest event for my area. She came because I had the number one unit in sales the previous year, and I won a night of her time in any city in the United States. I asked Mary Kay to come to Las Vegas. We held the event in Caesar's Palace trying to impress our founder. My dear friend Independent Elite Executive Senior

Sales Director Tracy Ley was then just beginning her Mary Kay business and was still singing and dancing in the Jubilee Show in the MGM Grand Hotel and Casino across the street from Caesar's Palace. After Mary Kay helped us with our guest event Tracy came over and sang to Mary Kay. In fact, Mary Kay spoke the words as Tracy sang, "Welcome to Our World." It was quite a duet. It was so exciting to have Mary Kay there in Las Vegas with most of the Fortenberry Area at the time. People in my area flew in from all over the country to spend the time with Mary Kay, and we had a great celebration. We took Mary Kay to see Tracy along with some of her team members perform as genuine Las Vegas showgirls in the Jubilee Show. Mary Kay loved it all. With all the responsibility she had, she still knew how to have a good time.

Mary Kay was always so gracious with her time. Whenever our group had events in Dallas, Mary Kay would always accept an invitation to speak to us and mentor our people. I always took notes whenever she spoke, and I still have those notes today. What I admired most was that she would stand there for hours getting her picture taken with each Sales Director. Even though she must have taken millions of pictures in her lifetime, not a single director ever felt rushed through the process. Mary Kay would treat the last person in line just as graciously as she had the first person in line. She was a very classy lady with a very big heart.

Mary Kay was also a phenomenal speaker and motivator. She could relate to a crowd like no one I have ever met. There is a popular story among some of the people who have been associated with Mary Kay for some time. When registrations for Seminar exceeds the capaticity of the main arena a satellite arena is set up (usually called "Hall A"); the arena and Hall A are linked with big screens and cameras showing what is happening at each area. Mary Kay didn't want the people in Hall A to feel left out so she always spoke to them personally instead of talking to them on a screen from the arena. She stepped lively onto the stage from backstage and when she did, her skirt fell to the floor. She was left on stage in front of hundreds of people in her slip. Without hesitation she grabbed her skirt, pulled it up into place, looked at the crowd, and said, "Now how's that for an entrance!" Mary Kay was the epitome of grace and poise and she never ceased to amaze me. The speeches she gave to thousands came across like they were tailored for each person in the audience. Whether she was looking me in the eye or if I was in the middle of the audience, I always felt like she was talking just to me. That was the beauty of her sincerity, her eloquence, and her passion. Mary Kay gave this speech at one of the last Seminars before she suffered a stroke that took away her wonderful gift of speech. It is fitting to share as an example of what a magnificent communicator she was.

We're on the crest of the most exciting year in our Company history—and your life. Wonderful things are happening. We have just been named No. 214 in the *Fortune* 500 private company listings! And for the second time we are on the lists of "The 100 Best Companies to Work For in America" and "The 10 Best Companies for Women to Work For." Mary Kay has become the best-selling brand of facial skin care and color cosmetics in the United States. Retail sales reached more than

$1.5 billion in 1994, and when all of the figures are in for 1995, we hope to be close to $2 billion.

We now have more than 400,000 Consultants and 8,000 Directors, and we are in twenty-five countries. I hope it is as thrilling to you as it is to me to know that every minute of every hour around the clock, a skin care class is being held somewhere in the world. However, I will not be happy until every woman in the world is offered the Mary Kay opportunity.

One of the most important ways you can positively affect people is to encourage them to success. There's a beautiful story I want to share with you about the effect of encouragement:

Teddy Stallard certainly qualified as "one of the least" in school with musty, wrinkled clothes and uncombed hair. When Miss Thompson spoke to Teddy, he always answered in monosyllables. Unattractive, unmotivated and distant, he was just plain hard to like. Even though his teacher said she loved all in her class the same, down inside she wasn't being completely truthful. Whenever she marked Teddy's papers, she got a certain pleasure out of putting Xs next to the wrong answers; when she put the Fs at the top of the papers, she always did it with flair. She should have known better. She had Teddy's records, and she knew more about him than she wanted to admit. The records read:

* 1st grade. Teddy shows promise with his work and attitude, but poor home situation.

* 2nd grade. Teddy could do better. Mother is seriously ill. He receives little help at home.

* 3rd grade. Teddy is a good boy but too serious. He is a slow learner. His mother died this year.

* 4th grade. Teddy is very slow, but well behaved. His father shows no interest.

Christmas came, and the boys and girls in Miss Thompson's class brought her Christmas presents. Among the presents was one from Teddy wrapped in brown paper and held together with Scotch tape. On the paper were written the simple words, "For Miss Thompson from Teddy." When she opened Teddy's present, out fell a gaudy rhinestone bracelet with half the stones missing and a bottle of cheap perfume. The other boys and girls began to giggle and smirk over Teddy's gifts, but Miss Thompson had the sense to silence them by immediately putting on the bracelet and some of the perfume. Holding her wrist up for the other children to smell, she said, "Doesn't it smell lovely?" The children, taking their cue from the teacher, readily agreed with "oohs" and "ahs." At the end of the day, Teddy lingered behind. He slowly walked to his teacher's desk and said softly, "Miss Thompson ... Miss Thompson, you smell just like my mother ... and her bracelet looks real pretty on you, too. I'm glad you like my presents." When Teddy left, Miss Thompson got down on her knees and asked God to forgive her. The next day the children were welcomed by a new teacher. Miss Thompson had become a different person. She was no longer just a teacher; she had become an agent of God. She was now a person committed to loving her children and doing things for them that would live on after her. She helped all the children, but especially the slow ones ... and especially Teddy Stallard. By the end of the school year, Teddy showed dramatic improvement. He had caught up with most of the students and was even ahead of some. She didn't hear from Teddy for a long time. Then one day, she received a note that read:

Dear Miss Thompson,
I wanted you to be the first to know. I will be graduating second in my class.

Love,
Teddy Stallard

Four years later, another note came:

Dear Miss Thompson,
They just told me I will be graduating first in my class. I wanted you to be the first to know. The university has not been easy, but I liked it.

Love,
Teddy Stallard

And four years later:

Dear Miss Thompson,
As of today, I am Theodore Stallard, M.D. How about that?
I wanted you to be the first to know. I am getting married
next month—the 27th to be exact. I want you to come and sit
where my mother would sit if she were alive. You are the only
family I have now. Dad died last year.

Love,
Teddy Stallard

Miss Thompson went to that wedding and sat where Teddy's mother would have sat. She deserved to sit there; she had done something for Teddy that he could never forget.

Now, to accomplish your own personal dream, you need to be focused. First of all, keep your goals in front of you daily—in the bathroom, on your desk, on the refrigerator, on the sun visor of your car. Follow through to develop them into your month-end reality. Make 20/20 (20 skincare classes in a month) a way of life. Make a commitment to continuity. You have already heard the amazing statistics that have come from those who have followed through on 20/20. The average sales have been from $2,000 to $5,000 a month and many have five recruits from that month. It is true that every success begins at the skin care class.

Remember that the speed of the leader is the speed of the gang. So get committed to your mission. So committed that it doesn't matter what's happening around you. Be commitment-based and action-oriented. When you have a purpose and a passion, you have the ability to rise out of the ashes time and time again. Pick your passion and work like this is more than a career, because it really is. It is a way of life. I ask you this: How great can you allow yourself to be? Former General Colin Powell, in his speech announcing his decision not to run for president said, "You must have a passion to run the race and a quest to win."

Your mission will be to help grow your unit to its next size of achievement... fifty or seventy-five or one hundred or one hundred and twenty-five. This can happen for you as you get each of your unit members to join the 20/20 Club, because the skin care class is where those new business associates will be found.

> So now is the time to start anew.
> To dream big dreams that will come true.
> Set your goal for what you'll do.
> Make a promise, follow through.
> Your dreams come true with Mary Kay.
> With great rewards along the way.
> You'll succeed, you know how.
> Starting here starting now.
> So whatever you wish, whatever you dream,
> Whatever you hope to achieve.
> Whatever you try for, whatever you plan
> It's yours if you'll only believe.

The last Mary Kay Seminar that Mary Kay Ash was able to attend was a very touching and important evening in my business and in my life. The stroke had left Mary Kay unable to speak but she still wanted to spread her message of encour-

agement to all of the people that came to Seminar. In true
Mary Kay fashion, she wrote a speech and allowed me to
accompany her on stage and read the speech she had written.
It was a powerful moment and she showed to the end that
what your mind can conceive and your heart truly believes you
can achieve. This is an excerpt from the Mary Kay's speech
that I read on her behalf.

What more could any woman ask for?

To be surrounded by all of you, to feel and to hear all
of your love, to know the great joy I feel standing here
today.

I am convinced I must have done something right! I must
have done the job that God intended for me. It is true,
I did have the dream. I did see the vision. I did provide
you the vehicle. And for thirty-four years I have watched
with such pride because you just took my dream and this
opportunity and you ran with it,

And you will continue to run with it because there are so
many women who will want to follow your great example.
Believe me, we have so many lives yet to touch, (his work
will never be finished, Never. Never. Never.

I have said before that great leaders are forming in our
sales force, and you can see some of them standing here
with me today. There are also great leaders at the company—caring, committed employees who have learned
very well how to do things the Mary Kay way.

I am so blessed by each of you who are inspired by my
example. Today, I would like to think that you can use my

example and let it inspire you to become your own best example. It is so simple. When you understand the big picture of what we are about, then and only then are you fully capable of being the best you can be and inspiring others.

Thank you from the bottom of a grateful heart for allowing me to touch your lives. Now it's your turn to run with your dreams and touch more lives than I ever imagined! You can do it! *I love you.*

I have been blessed in my life that I found both the Mary Kay business opportunity and made so many friends through my business. But the one who has changed my life the most was my friend Mary Kay Ash. I will always miss and love you, Mary Kay.

I would like to thank each person who has taken the time to read this book—thank you from the bottom of my grateful heart. I can only hope that there was something in these pages that found a way to touch your life. If so, allow me to give you the same advice Mary Kay gave me and thousands of others:

Now it is your turn to run with your dreams and touch more lives. Pass it on.

HONORING OFFSPRING INDEPENDENT NATIONAL SALES DIRECTORS

IN ORDER OF DEBUT DATES

Independent Senior National
Sales Director
Johnnette Shealy

Independent Senior National
Sales Director
Linda McBroom

Independent Executive National
Sales Director
Karlee Isenhart

Independent Senior National
Sales Director
Shirley Oppenheimer

Independent Senior National
Sales Director
Michelle Sudeth

Independent National
Sales Director
Kelly McCarroll

Independent National
Sales Director
Vicky Fuselier

Independent National
Sales Director
Kimberely Copeland

Independent Senior National
Sales Director
Scarlett Walker

Independent National
Sales Director
Rhonda Fraczkowski

Independent Senior National
Sales Director
Pamela Fortenberry-Slate

Independent National
Sales Director
Amy Dunlap

Independent National
Sales Director
Gena Gass

Independent National
Sales Director
Terri Schafer

Independent National
Sales Director
Donna Meixsell